Intuitive Tarot

31 Days to Learn to Read Tarot Cards and Develop Your Intuition

Written by: **Brigit Esselmont**

Illustrations by: **Ellie Moreing**

First Edition – September 2012 | Second Edition – October 2014 | Third Edition – October 2019

Version 3.0 © Copyright 2012-19 Brigit Esselmont

Learn to read Tarot cards from your heart, not the book

I'll show you how...

Hey there, Beautiful Soul!

I am thrilled that our paths have crossed!

You and I both know that nothing happens by accident. Whatever brought you here—whether it was because you're just starting out with Tarot or you've been reading for a while and want to hone your skills—I know it's for a very important reason.

Here's what I believe:

> **You are here because you're an intuitive soul and you're seeking to create an (even more) inspired life for yourself and others using Tarot as a guide. You're looking to connect with your inner wisdom and your intuition, to gather glimpses into your secret self and the ways in which you move in this world. And you want to grow and expand your Tarot reading skills so you can truly make an impact, even if it's only for yourself.**

Well, my friend, you're in the right place.

As I see it, Tarot is a powerful tool you can use to access your subconscious and tap into the wisdom and answers that reside in us all. You have this wisdom, too (even if you don't think of yourself as "intuitive" or "psychic"). Everyone does! And that's fantastic news because it means we have the power to take conscious control over our paths, using Tarot as our guide.

When you read Tarot, you'll gain insights into the direction your life is taking, find out where to invest your energy, and even discover what might be waiting for you around the corner. Whether you want to explore deep spiritual matters or dip into practical, day-to-day issues, the Tarot can help you access your inner wisdom to enrich your story.

For centuries, people have turned to the Tarot as a source of divination and guidance. And while many professional readers or self-proclaimed "gurus" would like us to believe it takes special psychic gifts or decades of intense study to use the Tarot, that's simply not true. (I suspect hinting at some ancient, hidden mysticism that only they can access is a ploy to sell their products and services!) Don't believe them for a second. In 31 days, you can have an in-depth understanding of the Tarot and its meanings and confidently read the cards, just like the professionals do, by following the step-by-step system in this book.

I designed Intuitive Tarot: 31 Days to Learn to Read Tarot Cards and Develop Your Intuition for people just like you. I have taken everything I've learned in my 20 years' experience as a professional Tarot reader and broken it down into one easy-to-use program. It's simple. It's doable. And, as you'll see in the pages to come, it's exciting, fun, and filled with "ah-ha!" moments.

How to Get the Most Out of This Book

Intuitive Tarot: 31 Days to Learn to Read Tarot Cards and Develop Your Intuition is divided into daily lessons and activities that you can work through at your own pace. Using this approach, you won't just learn how to read Tarot; you'll put those skills into practice right away.

Here's how it works...

For each day, you'll find a lesson breaking down an essential concept or technique, followed by a series of activities that show you how to turn the teaching into action. Read the lesson and then do the activities. It's that simple!

Before you start, I recommend you get yourself a fresh, blank journal that you'll record all of your activities and insights in over the next 31 days. You'll learn all about keeping a Tarot journal on Day 5, but trust me, you'll want somewhere to write everything you're discovering from Day 1!

Now, while I have designed this book as a 31-day program, you don't need to complete it in 31 days. Take it at your own pace. You might zip through it in under a month or space it out and do one lesson per week. Do what feels good to you. You may find you prefer to do some activities more than once— or, even better, make them a part of your daily Tarot practice (the "Card of the Day" activity comes to mind!).

Remember, learning Tarot isn't a do-it-once-and-you're-done thing; it's a rewarding, fulfilling, lifelong adventure. This book will get you started as quickly as possible, but where you go from here is entirely up to you. I can't wait to see what you discover!

OK, so are you ready to dive in? Let's do this!

You're Invited to Join the Biddy Tarot Community for Only $1

Discover how to become a more confident, intuitive tarot reader inside the Biddy Tarot Community, with over 1500+ Tarot Lovers.

Inside the Community, you can:

- Practice reading Tarot for others on the Free Tarot Reading platform
- Join in the forum conversation with 1500+ Tarot enthusiasts
- Get answers to all of your questions as you develop your Tarot reading skills
- Learn from 25+ Tarot Topics and Masterclasses
- Access 50+ Tarot resources including spreads, charts and worksheets
- Boost your Tarot reading confidence and connect with your Tarot tribe

As a special thank-you for reading Intuitive Tarot and including me on your Tarot journey, you're invited to join the #1 online Tarot community for just $1 for 14 days.

Get started today at biddytarot.com/community-trial.

About Brigit

Brigit Esselmont is the best-selling author of Everyday Tarot (**everydaytarot.com**) and The Ultimate Guide to Tarot Card Meanings (**biddytarot.com/ ultimate-guide**) and founder of Biddy Tarot , **biddytarot.com**. As an intuitive entrepreneur, Brigit has helped millions of people all around the world discover how to trust their intuition, access their inner power, and draw the Divine into their everyday life, using Tarot as a guide.

On a mission to bring Tarot out of the closet and into the mainstream, Brigit believes that Tarot is a modern, intuitive tool for purpose-driven people who are ready to live life at their fullest potential – no crystal balls or crushed velvet required. When she's not teaching, coaching, or flipping Tarot cards, Brigit loves spending time with her two daughters and husband on the Sunshine Coast, Australia.

Brigit believes anyone can read Tarot. It's all about saying "Yes!" to your intuition and trusting that you already have the answers within you.

Let's Stay in Touch

I love connecting with intuitively inspired, purpose-driven people who read Tarot. So, let's stay in touch! Access our free Tarot resources and Tarot card meanings at **biddytarot.com.**

And follow me on Instagram (**instagram.com/biddytarot**) where I share Tarot tips, spreads, practice opportunities and more Tarot goodness. Be part of the growing tribe who are making Tarot and intuition part of their everyday life – and don't forget to tag me **@biddytarot** and **#biddytarot** with your own Tarot pics and insights!

Intuitive Tarot Daily Lesson Calendar

1	2	3	4	5	6	7
What is the Tarot?	But First... Choose your Tarot Deck	Cleanse and Care for your Tarot Deck	Get to Know Your Tarot Cards	Start Your Tarot Journal	How to Learn the Tarot Card Meanings	Learn About the Minor Arcana

8	9	10	11	12	13	14
Learn About the Suit of Cups	Learn About the Suit of Pentacles	Learn About the Suit of Swords	Learn About the Suit of Wands	Learn About the Court Cards	Learn About the Major Arcana	Learn Tarot by Numbers

15	16	17	18	19	20	21
Interpret the Symbolism in the Tarot	Interpret the Stories in the Cards	Meditation with the Tarot	A Card a Day	Good Cards, Bad Cards	Reversed Cards	Create Tarot Card Combos

22	23	24	25	26	27	28
Create the Sacred Space	Ask Powerful Questions	Choosing a Tarot Spread	Do a Tarot Reading	Discover the Celtic Cross	Reading Tarot for Yourself	Reading Tarot for Others

29	30	31
Reflect and Ask for Feedback	Help! What If...	Trust Your Intuition

Table of Contents

Section 1: Getting Started
(Days 1 to 5)

Ready. Set. Tarot!
Here's everything you need
to get started.

Day 1: What is the Tarot?

So, what is the Tarot, anyway? Arthur Edward Waite, co-creator of the well-known Rider Waite deck, described it this way:

> **The Tarot embodies symbolical presentations of universal ideas, behind which lie all the implicits of the human mind, and it is in this sense that they contain secret doctrine, which is the realization by the few of truths imbedded in the consciousness of all, though they have not passed into express recognition by ordinary men.**

My perspective is much simpler: The Tarot is the storybook of our lives, the mirror to our souls, and the key to unlocking our inner wisdom. It's an invitation to your subconscious mind and an opportunity to tap into the knowledge and answers that reside in us all.

These 78 cards capture every spiritual lesson we encounter in our lives, and when we consult the Tarot, we receive the exact lessons we need to learn (and master) to live an inspired life. It's beautiful and exciting and, sometimes, a little intimidating.

The traditional Tarot deck has 78 cards, divided into the Major Arcana and the Minor Arcana (including the Court Cards). The 22 cards of the Major Arcana reflect the vital spiritual lessons we face throughout our lives. Their energy is 'big', and these cards often have profound, karmic impacts on us. The Major Arcana cards are also associated with the archetypal qualities present in our individual worlds, both within and without. These archetypes are the understood symbols or patterns of behavior that flow through from the collective to the individual, from the universe around us to the universe inside us.

The remaining 56 cards form the Minor Arcana and represent the characters, events, and circumstances that impact our daily lives. The Minor Arcana is made up of four suits: Cups, Pentacles, Swords, and Wands. Ten numbered cards comprise each suit, from the Ace to the Ten, along with four court cards: The Page, Knight, Queen and King. The court cards specifically relate to the people or personalities within our lives.

To do a Tarot reading, you simply need to ask a question, shuffle and lay out the cards, and then interpret what they mean for you (more on that in Lesson 6).

Many people turn to the Tarot with questions about their relationships, career, finances, personal development, day-to-day situations, and significant life transitions – and so can you! The cards won't tell you exactly what will happen or offer specific details, like "You'll meet your future husband on the evening of August 16," but they can give you insight into where you might be heading.

Best of all, the Tarot shows you how to make positive changes NOW so you can manifest your goals and your dreams in the future.

Where Does Tarot Come From?

Contrary to popular belief, the Tarot did not originate with the Ancient Egyptians. It started as a card game called Tarrochi in the 1500s. Tarot became more widely known in the 1700s, mostly as an occult tool, a label that then solidified in the early 1900s when English occultist and Golden Dawn member, Aleister Crowley, created the Thoth Tarot deck. Later, Arthur Edward Waite co-created the Rider Waite Tarot deck, bringing us to Tarot as we know it today.

With the evolution of the collective consciousness in the 1960s, Tarot use likewise evolved. People started applying it to their personal development as much as divination, ascribing psychological meanings to the cards.

And yet, despite the fact that many were using it more and more to learn about themselves, the media continued to portray the Tarot as a mysterious tool. The 'fortune telling' characterization stuck and, unfortunately, kept this amazing source of intelligence out of the hands of many who could have benefited from it.

I'm glad to say we've come a long way since then. Today, there are thousands of different decks created by a range of incredible artists, bringing new and gorgeous expressions to the ancient wisdom of Tarot.

Now, everyone can access a Tarot deck that resonates with them, to guide them in any area of life – from creating careers that light them up to supporting those they love and engaging in self-reflection and soul searching. Tarot has finally arrived in the mainstream, and I'm a big advocate for that!

So, How Does Tarot Work?

Is it divine magic? Frivolous entertainment? The work of the devil?

I'm glad you asked.

The truth is we don't know how the Tarot works. At least, not exactly. And really, it comes down to how you want it to work and how you wish to incorporate Tarot in your life. Because ultimately, the Tarot is a tool, and it's up to you how you'll use it.

But I'm getting ahead of myself. Here's what I believe:

> **The Tarot reflects back to us what we already know within ourselves, our inner wisdom.**

We may already consciously perceive the insight we receive in a Tarot reading, in which case, the reading can be a heartening confirmation or affirmation. Or, we might be entirely unaware of the message... until now. It's as if the Tarot cards create an instant connection to our subconscious minds so we can access what we already know deep within and bring it into our conscious awareness and, from there, take action.

Of course, that doesn't quite explain what happens when you're reading for another person, and you pick up that they're dating someone twenty years their junior – something they have told no one about up to that point (true story!). What's happening there?

Well, here is where things might be a little more 'out there' and magical. You see, I believe that we are all connected to collective, universal wisdom as well as our own inner wisdom. And when we read the Tarot cards and connect with our intuition, we can tap into this universal knowledge and then act as a conduit to share these intuitive messages with the people who need them.

(Are you still with me?!)

Now, whether all of this is the work of the devil... well, I'll let you decide that for yourself. But there's one thing I know for sure, and it's this: when I read Tarot, I couldn't be closer to God if I tried. Tarot has this beautiful way of connecting you to your truest wisdom, your inner sanctuary, your soul. And to me, that's where God resides.

Does Tarot Tell the Future?

It's a common assumption that the Tarot will predict your fate or spell out your destiny for you.

Want to know when you'll get married? Ask the Tarot!

Want to know if you'll get your dream job? Pull out those cards!

At least, that's what many people assume you can do with the Tarot cards.

Here's the thing. While you can use the Tarot cards to predict what might happen in the future, is that where you want to focus your attention and energy?

Think about it. Imagine the Tarot cards said, 'Awesome, you know that dream job you've always wanted? Well, go buy a bottle of champagne, because it's coming to you in August!' Would you still work as hard to get the job? Or would you relax because, hey, the job's already in the bag? And if you were more relaxed, do you expect you'd still get it, or would you have changed the outcome?

And what if you don't get the answer you want? What if the Tarot cards said, 'Hey, sorry, but there's no wedding on the horizon'? Would you give up on your dream to get married? (Or would you shop around until a Tarot reader gave you the response you were looking for?)

When you ask about the future, you're assuming it's all laid out in front of you and there's little that you can do to change it. Which is great if you get the answer you want, but not so great if you don't. And either way, believing that an outcome is 'locked in' means giving up your agency. YOU are the one who makes things happen, so why would you relinquish that awesome power?

The best way to predict your future is to create it.

While the Tarot cards can offer you insight into what might be around the corner, they are much more powerful when you use them to understand the present. When you can see your current influences, you'll be in a stronger position to shape your future. Wouldn't you prefer to feel empowered by the Tarot cards and your intuition than to be told what may or may not happen?

If you want to find out when you'll get married, focus on what actions you can take now to find the partner of your dreams and create a fulfilling, long-lasting relationship. And if you want to know if you'll get your dream job, look to the opportunities available to you today so you can manifest that dream job in the future.

I see the Tarot as a tool for understanding the present energies which will influence the future. I also believe in free will, so if you don't like where you're heading, then you should put in place strategies to create a more positive or desirable outcome. You may still be on a specific path or learning a particular lesson, but you can make your journey easier with the Tarot's help.

And, as I often say to my students, 'Forewarned is forearmed.' Some things might be unavoidable, but at least you'll be prepared.

Paulo Coelho says it perfectly in his book, The Alchemist:

> When people consult me, it's not that I'm reading the future; I am guessing at the future. The future belongs to God, and it is only he who reveals it, under extraordinary circumstances. How do I guess at the future? Based on the omens of the present. The secret is here in the present. If you pay attention to the present, you can improve upon it. And if you improve on the present, what comes later will also be better.

I believe the Tarot helps us see and interpret 'the omens of the present,' as well as the energies, buried emotions and beliefs, intuitive understanding, and the deep wisdom of our world and ourselves. But it's up to us to decide what we'll do with them.

How to Use Tarot in Your Everyday Life

So now you know that the Tarot cards are not just for fortune telling and predicting the future!

You can use Tarot for personal development, life coaching, business planning – you name it! There is no limit to how you can integrate the Tarot cards into your everyday life. And better yet, there is no one 'right way' for how to use the Tarot. All that matters is what feels resonant and in alignment to YOU.

Here's just a taste of how you can use the Tarot cards:

- Seek spiritual guidance
- Understand the present
- Learn more about yourself
- Explore mythology and symbolism
- Personal growth and development
- Have fun with your friends
- Solve problems or dilemmas
- Earn an income as a professional
- Make important decisions
- Confirm a gut feeling
- Connect with other people's energy
- Daily or weekly guidance
- Help others in emotional distress
- Self-examination and psychoanalysis
- Connect with your pets
- Empowerment
- Meditation and introspection

- Fortune telling and predicting the future
- Develop your psychic abilities or intuition
- Creative thinking

And that's just a handful of ideas. I have students, friends, and fellow readers – not to mention the Biddy Tarot Community (**biddytarot.com/ community-trial**)– who offer up new and innovative ways to incorporate the Tarot in their lives. Let your imagination go wild and bring the cards to life!

Activities

1.1 Discover What Tarot Means to You

- What inspired you to learn Tarot?
- What role do you see Tarot playing in your life?

1.2 Set Your Tarot Goals

- By the end of these 31 days, what do you want to think, feel, and do when it comes to reading Tarot with confidence?
- Set a regular time in your calendar for learning and reading Tarot. (I recommend 30-60 minutes a day.)
- What other commitments do you need to make to yourself to complete this program?

1.3 Explore the Biddy Tarot Community

- Get your 14-day trial of the Biddy Tarot Community for only $1 at **biddytarot.com/community-trial/**
- Jump in and explore the Forums, Tarot Topics and Masterclasses

Day 2: But First... Choose Your Tarot Deck

If I were to ask you to picture a Tarot deck, what would you see? For many of us, the image in our minds would probably resemble the Rider Waite deck and its cast of characters: The Fool traipsing along a cliff's edge, a heart pierced by three Swords, a young Page startled by the fish popping out of his cup. But what if The Lovers were represented by a pair of geese? The Fool a woman dancing with abandon in a swirl of color and butterflies?

There are hundreds of different Tarot decks to choose from, all with their own symbolism, energy, stories, mythology, and artwork. Whether you're a Tarot beginner or a seasoned expert, choosing a Tarot deck can be overwhelming. So, where do you begin? How do you sift through the vast array of choices to find your ideal Tarot deck?

Here are nine sure-fire ways to select a deck that's perfect for you.

1. Look for a Personal and Intuitive Connection with the Cards

When choosing a Tarot deck, the most important thing is that you connect with it intuitively.

Your best friend might rave about the Wild Unknown deck, but if you break out in a sweat and go blank every time you do a Tarot reading with those cards, then it's not the right deck for you.

And if your Tarot teacher swears by the Rider Waite deck, but you're in love with the Fairy Tarot Cards, then go with the Fairy Tarot Cards. As we'll discuss shortly, that intuitive connection is powerful.

If you've got a new age shop or bookstore nearby, go to the store and touch the cards - handle every deck on display. Which deck caught your eye first? What energy do you pick up as you hold the cards in your hand? Which ones feel good? Is there a personal connection between you and the Tarot cards? Do you find you keep returning to a particular deck? Which deck do you NOT want to set down?

And if you're looking to buy your Tarot cards online, most of those questions still apply. Do a quick Google search and skim through the card images to see if you sense a connection. Did a particular deck capture your attention? Are there any you find especially beautiful? Do you find your emotions stirring or even physical sensations arising in your body? That's always a good sign!

2. Explore the Imagery of Each Card

Next, explore every card. (If you're viewing the deck online, find as many images as possible via Google or even Instagram.)

What is your first reaction to the images? Do you like the colors and patterns? Are you drawn to the artwork? Are there other variations of the deck that catch your eye? For example, I much prefer the Radiant Rider Waite deck to the traditional Rider Waite deck for its bright colors.

Also, can you get a sense for the meaning of each card? Explore both the Major and Minor Arcana. In decks like the Tarot de Marseilles, the Minor Arcana cards do not have the same imagery and 'story' as the Rider Waite deck, for example. If you get an intuitive sense of the cards' meanings when you're exploring a deck, move that deck to your shortlist.

3. Consider Your Experience Level

The Rider Waite deck is popular, and with good reason: it's easy to understand, the imagery is straightforward and practical, and there's a tremendous amount of information available for this deck. If you're new to Tarot, it's a great starter deck.

That said, don't limit yourself by thinking that, as a newbie, you can only read with the Rider Waite deck. There may be other decks with which you have a stronger connection. Remember: that intuitive relationship comes first!

4. Decide If You Want to Go Traditional or Modern

Are you fascinated by the traditional Tarot decks, like the Tarot de Marseilles, the Visconti Tarot, or the Original Rider Waite Tarot deck? Or are you drawn to the modern (and often independent) Tarot decks, such as the Wild Unknown, Fountain Tarot, Lumina Tarot, and Starchild Tarot?

I LOVE the new decks emerging on the market right now. The artwork is beautiful, and the imagery is relevant to our current times. (When was the last time you saw a knight roaming the streets?!)

You can view all of these decks and more at **biddytarot.com/decks**, to see all the different options and get an idea of what type of deck resonates with you.

5. Review the 'Little White Book'

Most Tarot decks will come with a guidebook explaining the imagery and the Tarot card meanings. However, some decks have more information than others – and some may have no instruction at all!

If you prefer knowing exactly what a card means and why, then make sure you check out what I like to call the 'little white book' that comes with the deck to see if it gives you what you need. Do you like the writing? The tone? Do you enjoy the approach the deck's creators took to it? If the accompanying guide isn't enough, go online to find a blog or eBook that explains the cards in more detail.

And if you are quite happy interpreting the Tarot cards via your intuition and energetic connection, well, then having no book at all might be a blessing!

6. Choose Quality Over Price

Most Tarot cards will be nice and thick to ensure that you can continue using them for many years.

However, beware of cheaper, lower-quality reproductions. The colors may bleed, the cardboard may be flimsy and tear easily, or the cards can be more prone to damage (and unlikely to withstand the test of time and love and frequent shuffling). Read the reviews online and avoid the poor quality decks, especially if you plan on using them regularly.

7. Don't Be Afraid to Buy Your Own Tarot Cards

There's a rumor going around that Tarot cards should only ever be gifted to you and that you can't buy your own. Well, phooey!

I would much prefer to buy a Tarot deck that I know is a perfect fit than wait around for someone to gift me a deck of their choosing – what if it feels 'off'? What if there's no intuitive connection? So, don't hesitate to buy your Tarot deck! (Of course, there's nothing to stop you from dropping a few hints at Christmas or birthday time about the decks you love the most...)

My Recommended Tarot Decks

To help you get started, here are a few Tarot decks I recommend. You can explore all of these decks in more detail at **biddytarot.com/decks**:

Everyday Tarot – I created this modern deck with Eleanor Grosch, a brilliant illustrator known for her bold and colorful designs. It's a take on the popular Rider Waite, with simplified colors (purple, gold, and white), stories, and symbolism so that you can focus on what's most important. It's perfect for beginners and more advanced readers. Everyday Tarot is also the deck we feature on the Biddy Tarot website.

Radiant Rider Waite – This deck is a brightly colored version of the traditional Rider Waite deck, and it's fabulous for learning Tarot. I cannot recommend it enough. It doesn't have to be the only deck you buy, of course, but I consider it an excellent place for getting started.

Gaian Tarot – An earth-based healing deck with imagery that's easy to read and interpret.

The Lumina Tarot – A modern and absolutely gorgeous adaptation of the Rider Waite deck.

Remember, it's OK to change Tarot decks later. In fact, many Tarot readers choose from a variety of decks, depending on who is sitting across the table or even on how they're feeling that day (there's that intuitive connection again!).

I use the Everyday Tarot and the Radiant Rider Waite for teaching, but when reading for myself, I like to change things up according to my mood and the question I'm asking. I often have a 'deck of the month' – a particular Tarot deck I'm loving and exploring, all within the safety of my personal readings.

Tarot vs. Oracle Decks

As you're choosing your first deck, be sure to choose a Tarot deck rather than an Oracle deck.

What's the difference? Tarot decks tend to have a similar structure: 78 cards with 22 Major Arcana cards and 56 Minor Arcana cards. And while the visual elements vary between Tarot decks, you'll typically find a consistent 'essence' across all decks.

Oracle decks, on the other hand, are more free flowing. There are no structures or common meanings, no set number of cards. Oracle decks draw from multiple sources of inspiration – angels, goddesses, positive affirmations, poets, and so on.

In a reading, I find that Oracle cards highlight the core themes or energies present, whereas the Tarot cards give more detail about what's happening and why. So, although you can use Tarot and Oracle decks together in beautiful ways, we'll be focusing only on the Tarot in this guide. So, make sure you choose a Tarot deck!

Activity

2.1 Buy Your Tarot Deck

- If you haven't already, buy your first Tarot deck!

Day 3: Cleanse and Care for Your Tarot Deck

Now, you've brought home your new Tarot deck. You've unwrapped the cellophane, popped open the box, maybe even shuffled the cards once or twice. Time to read some Tarot, right? Well, maybe not just yet. I want to teach you the powerful way I love to mark a new deck's 'homecoming.'

Here's the thing about Tarot – it's all about energy. There's energy in you and in your cards. Your readings carry their own energy, too. So, if you want to create a crystal-clear Tarot reading, it's essential that you're working with crystal-clear energy. And that all starts with cleansing your Tarot deck and infusing it with all your good vibes!

So, let's talk about when to cleanse your deck and how to do it.

When to Cleanse Your Tarot Deck

You'll need to cleanse your Tarot deck the very first time you buy it, especially if it's a pre-owned deck. Remember, decks carry energy. And since you want to make sure that your deck holds *your* energy, rather than someone else's, give your cards a thorough energy 'scrub' before you use them.

Now, while that initial cleanse is one of the most important, it's not the only one. You will probably find that you need to cleanse your deck again from time to time as you continue to read with it. (We never need to clean anything just once, do we?) There are no hard and fast rules about when to clear your deck; you've got to trust your intuition about what your cards need. Sometimes a quick shuffle is enough to shake loose any stuck energy. Other times, a full moon bath is called for.

Generally, you'll know when it's time to cleanse your Tarot deck. You'll have that niggling sense that something isn't quite right with the connection between you and your cards. Here are a few examples:

- You or your Tarot cards may have been exposed to a lot of negative energy (for example, a particularly negative client or a challenging situation in your personal life).

- Your Tarot readings are confusing and unclear, and you are often drawing a blank with the cards.

- Other people have touched your cards without your permission.

- Your cards have fallen on the floor or had an accident.

- You haven't used your Tarot cards for quite some time, and you want to reconnect with them.

- You've had a major personal transformation and wish to refresh your deck with your new energy.

- It's a full moon, and you want to make the most of its powerful energy.

And finally, sometimes it just feels like now is the right time for a cleanse.

How to Cleanse Your Tarot Deck

There are lots of different ways to clear negative energy and cleanse your Tarot deck. The important thing is to choose the techniques that feel right to you and to the situation (e.g., you might use one method in between each reading and another only seasonally or once a year).

Here are a few ways you can clear and cleanse your Tarot deck:

Sorting and Shuffling

First, sort your cards in order, starting with the Major Arcana, then into each of the suits of the Minor Arcana. As you do, glance at each card and remember the special message it has to offer you in your readings. (If this is your first full trip through your deck, note any intuitive hits you have about the meaning or message in the cards.)

You can also use this time to check that you have every card in your deck (a few years back, I found that I had been missing the Ace of Swords without even realizing it!).

Once your cards are sorted and in order, start shuffling and reinvigorating your cards with your energy. You might like to shuffle seven times, put your cards in a big messy pile and randomly select cards, or use a shuffling technique that's comfortable to you. The key here is that you're not doing these activities mindlessly; you're doing them intentionally, to let your cards 'breathe' and be.

Knocking or Tapping the Deck

A quick way to release any stuck energy in between readings is to knock or tap the deck three times while also visualizing that stuck energy getting rapped loose – like knocking packed dirt off the soles of your shoes. It's particularly helpful if you've had an intense reading or the energy afterward felt unresolved.

Meditation

Hold your cards in both hands, close your eyes, and relax. Allow your mind to sit quietly, free of any thought, and just 'be' with your cards. You may then want to visualize the Universal energy drawing itself through you and into your cards, surrounding the deck in a protective white light. Those with an understanding of Reiki may enjoy channeling their healing Reiki energy through the cards. This technique is my favorite, as it's easy to do in between readings and helps me focus and concentrate on my next client.

Moon Bath

The full moon is an exquisite source of energy for your cards. When the moon is full, you can place your cards in a window or even outside to bathe in its light. Alternatively, many people use this time to conduct a special ritual or to cite different incantations for cleansing their Tarot cards.

Smudge Stick

Burn dried sage or rosemary (or use a store-bought smudge stick) and pass the cards through the smoke several times. You can also cleanse any crystals you use during the process in the same way.

Salt Burial

Many cultures consider salt to be a powerful cleansing agent, and you can use it to draw negative energy out from your cards. First, wrap your Tarot deck in a plastic bag as tightly as you can, squeezing out as much air as possible before sealing the bag. Then take an airtight container that is larger than your Tarot deck, place your wrapped cards inside, and then encircle your cards with salt on all sides, above and below. It is imperative that you use an airtight container as the salt will not only gather the energies from the Tarot deck but also any moisture that might be in the air, potentially damaging your cards. Keep your wrapped deck buried in the salt for at least a few days, or even a week, before taking them out and disposing of the salt.

Fresh Air

You know how good it feels to step outside just after a rain shower and breathe deep? Or to soak in the sun, enjoying its warmth on your skin? Well, your cards love it, too! Place your Tarot deck outside to take in the fresh air and draw in the sun's cleansing rays. Of course, keep in mind the practicalities and be careful not to set them out on a windy day!

Elemental Clearing

Elemental clearing calls each of the four elements into alignment with your deck's energy. For example:

- Earth clearing, use the salt burial
- Water clearing, bathe your cards in moonlight or sprinkle them with a little water
- Fire clearing, pass your cards over a candle
- Air clearing, use a smudge stick

You may even like to engage all four elements for a comprehensive cleanse and re-charge.

Storing Your Tarot Cards

Where are your cards going to 'live' in your house? Have you given any thought to where they'll sit when you're not using them? If not, now's a great time to do so! Here are a few ideas on how to store your cards:

Store your cards with a quartz crystal, which is a wonderful absorber of energies. You can use any of the cleansing techniques above if you want to keep your crystal 'clean' too.

- Place your Tarot cards at a specially made altar in between readings.
- Use baby wipes to remove any dust or stickiness from your cards.

- Keep your Tarot cards wrapped in a special cloth or stored in a unique Tarot box. Different colors have different vibrations, so choose a color that best suits your needs.

The rule of thumb is to remember that your Tarot cards are very special and treat them accordingly. The love and attentiveness you show your cards will only deepen the intuitive connection you share.

Activity

3.1 Cleanse Your Tarot Deck

- Whether you have just bought a new Tarot deck or you've had one collecting dust on the shelf, use any of the techniques above to cleanse your deck. Make it a regular practice from here on out. Now is also a superb time to choose a special place to store your cards.

Day 4: Get to Know Your Tarot Cards

The very first step in learning to read Tarot is to get acquainted with your deck! It's important to familiarize yourself with each card because it helps you to strengthen your intuitive bond and connect with the imagery and energy of the cards in a meaningful way.

Here are three fantastic ways to get to know your cards.

1. Explore Each Card

To start, move through your deck, one card at a time, and spend a few seconds with each as you take in its imagery, colors, and symbols, and repeat its name (hint: it's usually printed on the card!). Set your intention to connect with the deck's overall energy.

Then, go through the cards again, but this time, spend at least a few minutes with each one. Study it; pay attention to the details tucked in its corners. What's happening in the card? Note, too, how you feel as you examine each one. What sensations stir up in you? You might even find that you love some cards and despise others. Pay attention to all of this juicy information.

- Major Arcana: repeat the name of the card in your mind as you examine the image.

- Minor Arcana: find the principal symbol of the Cup, Pentacle, Sword or Wand. Note that in these cards, the card number typically corresponds with the number of those symbols within the card (e.g., the Two of Cups features two cups).

- Court cards: note how the Page, Knight, Queen, and King look. What similarities (if any) do they share? How do they differ? Can you get a sense of their personalities just by looking at them?

Repeat this process until you can select a card at random, recognize it and name it straight away.

2. Weave Together Groups of Cards

Now another interesting way of connecting with your Tarot deck is to observe how the cards flow from one to the next when you group them. For example, pull out all the Major Arcana cards and put them in order, from the Fool all the way through to the World. How do the story and imagery from one card lead into the next? Keep an eye out, too, for any patterns or symbols shared across the cards.

What's beautiful about this practice is that you'll start to see how the cards interact with each other and how the energy flows. It gives you more insight into what individual cards might mean, knowing where they fit in the context of the other cards.

You can do this practice for the Minor Arcana cards, as well, either grouping the cards by their suits or the numbers (e.g., all the Twos together). Again, watch for the themes and patterns across these cards as you group them.

We'll do more of this as we explore the different groups of cards later in this book.

3. Start Reading with the Cards

Finally, start reading the cards. I recommend drawing one Tarot card a day (I'll show you how to do that on Day 19) and using this practice to get 'up close and personal' with your new deck.

Remember: Getting to Know Your Deck Takes Time

Don't be surprised if you can't remember all the Tarot cards straight away. It can take weeks, months, or even years to recall or recognize all the cards.

What's more, some cards take a while to appear in your readings and tend to take a back seat, while other cards continually reappear, falling out of the deck and coming up in every reading you do.

This happened to me. I had been using my Tarot cards for personal readings and study for two years, and while I believed I had familiarized myself with all 78 Tarot cards, I soon realized there were cards I had never given much attention. Suddenly, the Five of Swords cropped up in a reading, and I thought, 'Where did you come from??' I hardly recognized it and was surprised to find a card with which I was so unacquainted. So, I used that reading as an opportunity to get much closer to the Five of Swords and understand its significance on both a general level and a personal one.

Interview Your Tarot Deck

As each deck you work with will have different energies, strengths, and limitations, it's important to 'interview' each one before working with it for the first time. It's a fun way to get insights into this particular deck – like, say, how does the Lumina Tarot differ from the Fountain Tarot – and how you will work best together. It's also a great way to find out what types of readings this deck will be best suited for (for example, you may choose to use one deck for career readings and another for relationship readings). The best way to find out where your deck shines is to ask it!

How to Interview Your Tarot Deck:

- Set aside a time where you won't be interrupted. Allow yourself at least thirty minutes to spend with your deck. (Trust me, this time is well worth it and will make every reading with this deck far more powerful.)

- Create a sacred space for you and your deck to enjoy. Light your favorite candles, surround yourself with crystals, play music that feels like it fits this deck. Or, take your deck out into nature and allow the elements to add a bit of magic. Make sure you bring your pen and a journal so you can capture your insights.

- Hold your deck in your hands, close your eyes, and take three deep breaths to center yourself. Or, listen to my Confidence Booster Meditation to ground your energy into the reading. You can download it for free at **biddytarot.com/meditate**.

- Shuffle the cards and lay them out according to the Tarot Deck Interview Spread on page 31

- Journal on each question and card, noting the sensations each one stirs up in you. What do you think it's telling you in response to each query? Note anything that stands out to you – imagery, colors, symbolism, or synchronicities between the cards you pulled.

- At the close of your 'interview', thank your deck for collaborating with you and welcome in many more beautiful readings together!

Tarot Deck Interview Spread

- Why have you come into my life at this time?
- What are your key strengths?
- What limitations do I need to be aware of?
- What are you here to teach me?
- How can we work together to deliver intuitive, confident readings?
- What is the highest potential of our collaboration?

Activity

4.1 Get to Know Your Tarot Deck

- Go through the process of familiarizing yourself with each of the Tarot cards.
- Test yourself: see how quickly you can find the following cards in your deck:

  - Seven of Swords
  - Nine of Pentacles
  - Queen of Cups
  - Chariot
  - Ace of Wands

- Interview your deck

  - Using the Tarot Deck Interview spread (see next page)

Tarot Deck Interview Spread

2
What are your key strengths?

1
Why have you come into my life at this time?

3
What limitations do I need to be aware of?

4
What are you here to teach me?

5
How can we work together to deliver intuitive, confident readings?

6
What is the highest potential of our collaboration?

Day 5: Start Your Tarot Journal

Want to know the secret to becoming an intuitive and confident Tarot reader? It's all about creating a personal and intuitive connection with your Tarot cards. And one of the most effective ways to do that is by keeping a Tarot journal.

Imagine, a place where you can record your readings, confirm your intuitive hits, create your own Tarot card meanings, and ultimately, form an intimate relationship with the Tarot and your intuition. That's your Tarot journal! More than that, I picture a Tarot journal as an ongoing conversation between you and the cards, one that gets more and more fascinating the more you interact.

Why You NEED to Keep a Tarot Journal

If you're like nearly every other Tarot reader I know, you want to read Tarot from the heart, not the book. And to do this, you realize that you need to put down the guide and learn how to connect on a personal and innate level with the Tarot cards. But putting the book down can be a little scary, right?

That's why you need your own Tarot book. Your Tarot journal will help you establish your unique ways of working with the Tarot cards and put your intuition on speed dial.

And that's just scratching the surface of what's possible when you keep a Tarot journal consistently. Here are a few other benefits:

1. You can connect on a 'soul level' with the Tarot

The Tarot is so intensely personal. It goes way beyond any meaning you'll read about in a book. Instead, Tarot reaches deep into your heart and your soul if you allow it to – and when you commit to writing a Tarot journal, you permit yourself to experience the Tarot cards on a deep, personal level. You go beyond the book's meaning and discover what the cards mean to YOU. And that's so incredibly powerful.

What's more, as you begin to unlock your inner wisdom, you'll discover new aspects of yourself that can be profoundly healing, transformative, and enlightening. The Tarot becomes a part of you and a reflection of who you really are.

2. You can create your own library of Tarot card meanings

Sure, you can pull up the Tarot card meanings in your favorite book (you may like The Ultimate Guide to Tarot Card Meanings – check it out at **biddytarot.com/ultimate-tarot**). But the real magic comes when you collect your personal meanings of the Tarot cards.

Let's say the Five of Cups came up in a reading for your friend's failed relationship. Your intuition told you it wasn't about regret or loss like the book told you; it was all about building a bridge and getting over it! You go with your gut and... the result? Your friend is blown away! It was exactly what she needed to hear.

Now imagine you had a whole library of such meanings, which you've personally experienced or observed in your Tarot readings. No more robotic, generic or boring Tarot readings! Instead, your readings will be highly specific, insightful, and accurate – and people will line up out the door to have a reading with you!

3. You can validate (and increase) your intuitive hits

Learning how to trust your intuition can be a huge sticking point for many people who want to read Tarot. I mean, how do you know if that niggling thought during a Tarot reading is something or nothing at all?

By recording your readings in your Tarot journal and reflecting on them later, you'll see where your intuitive hits were bang-on or if they've missed the mark (and how you can improve).

For example, you might come across the Three of Wands in a reading about finding the love of your life. Intuitively, you get the impression that it's a sign you need to explore internet dating, but you're not sure. You record it in your Tarot journal anyway and come back to it a few months later only to realize that, whoa, you met your new boyfriend online!

With this kind of validation, you'll become a master at interpreting the signs and picking up on those intuitive hits.

4. You'll see your progress as a Tarot reader

Tarot is a lifelong journey. From the time you open your very first deck of cards to when you do your thousandth professional reading, you're continually learning.

Now, let's face it. There will be times as you learn where you feel overwhelmed and on the verge of giving up. You'll set down your cards one morning and then won't pick them up again for two months. But imagine if you've recorded your journey in your Tarot journal and you can flick through the pages and see how far you've come? It might just be the one thing that keeps you moving forward.

Think about it this way – if you want to create a personal and intuitive connection with the Tarot cards, can you afford NOT to have a Tarot journal?

Five Things to Include in Your Tarot Journal

1. YOUR Tarot Card Meanings

It's one thing to interpret the Tarot cards, and it's another to interpret the Tarot cards intuitively. The best way to do that, as we've discussed, is to personalize their meanings.

Don't merely rely on memorizing the meanings described in your favorite books or blogs.

As you work through this book, connect with each Tarot card, and write about it in your Tarot journal. Here's how.

You might describe the picture on the card or the energy you get from it. Or you might start to tell a story about the card. Let your intuition guide you, without judgment or editing.

Next, look the card up in your favorite book of Tarot card meanings (like The Ultimate Guide to Tarot Card Meanings. Find it at **biddytarot.com/ultimate-tarot**). Learn about the traditional meanings of the card and the symbols contained within its imagery. Take notes in your Tarot journal. What new information does this add to your intuitive sense of the card? (Don't worry if it's different. That's perfectly OK!)

Finally, recall a time in your life when you experienced the energy of this Tarot card and write your story. For example, if you are working with the Fool, you might write about your first day at your very first job, and how it seemed like a massive step into the unknown. Connect your experience to what you know about the Tarot card and watch it come to life.

Finally, don't treat this exercise as a 'one and done' venture; make it a practice to revisit, revise, and refine your meanings. Over time, you will have created your very own library of Tarot card meanings that are personal to you – and incredibly powerful in intuitive Tarot readings.

2. YOUR Tarot Readings

Every time you read Tarot for yourself or others, make sure you have your Tarot journal open, and you're ready to take notes.

Why? When we're reading the Tarot cards, we often filter out parts of the reading that don't seem relevant to us right now, instead only remembering what rang true. But as a result, we can often miss important messages that may not have made sense in the moment but could have been helpful later down the track.

So next time you do a Tarot reading, record the following in your journal:

- What question did you ask?
- What spread did you use?
- Which cards did you draw?
- What messages did you receive in the reading?
- What actions will you take as a result of the reading?

Be as descriptive as possible and remember to jot down all messages – even those that may not make sense at the time.

Then, after a few weeks or a few months, come back to your Tarot journal and review your notes: What do you know now that you didn't know then? What new information can you add to the reading? Would you read the cards differently, now that you've seen how they have played out in 'real' life?

Record all your new insights in your Tarot journal. This vital feedback loop will help to validate your intuition and develop your Tarot reading skills and, if you're journaling about the individual card meanings, add your new interpretations and experiences to your 'library'.

3. YOUR Tarot Spreads

I LOVE creating new Tarot spreads! It's one of the most compelling ways of answering a question with the Tarot cards because it's tailored just for you... or for that question!

If you love getting creative, too, then use your Tarot journal to keep track of all the beautiful Tarot spreads you create. You might also make a note of specific 'mini questions' you like to work into your Tarot readings. For example, I really dig the following:

- 'What might I experience if...'
- 'How am I in relationship with...'
- 'What is in alignment with my Highest Good?'
- 'How can I fulfill my potential in [XYZ situation]?'

Then, when you go to create your next Tarot spread, you've already got a 'bank' of questions you can use. It's as simple as that.

4. YOUR Tarot Card Images

It's time to get out your colored pencils and embrace your inner artist!

Start by drawing a chosen Tarot card in your journal. (Or, if you're utterly un-artistic like me, trace over it!)

As you draw, take note of all the different symbols in the card. It might surprise you to realize how many things you haven't noticed before (I nearly always find something new – even after two decades of reading Tarot!).

Once you've outlined your Tarot card in your journal, then pull out your pencils... or your brush pens... or your watercolors... and start bringing your drawing to life. Maybe you'll stick to the color scheme you see in your Tarot deck. Or, maybe you'll paint with the eyes of your inner self, intuitively choosing the palette for each card.

Have fun with this! Create joyfully! (Adult coloring books are popular for a reason, after all – they're a blast!) Engage in the process and see how you begin to connect deeply with each card as you draw and color it in. Add color and embellishment to your heart's content!

5. YOUR Creative Writing

If the idea of drawing and painting Tarot cards has you hiding in a corner, you might prefer to use your creative writing skills to connect with your cards instead.

Choose a card, pull out a pen or pencil (pick a nice one that feels good), and get writing! You can keep it simple by 'free writing' for a certain length of time. No need to overthink it – just set the timer and away you go. Commit to writing non-stop, even if it's to say, 'I have no idea what to write!' Soon, your creative flow will kick in, and you may be surprised at your insights.

You can also opt to tell a story about what's happening in the Tarot card:

- Who is the character in the card?
- Where did they come from?
- What are their dreams and aspirations?
- What are they doing?
- What will they do next?
- Who do they meet along their journey?
- What lessons will they learn?

Or, you could choose five, ten, or even twenty Tarot cards and treat each one as page in a storybook. Create an entire story, from the first card to the last.

Again, have fun with it! Get your creative juices flowing, and soon, your intuition will also be along for the ride!

Activity

5.1 Start Your Tarot Journal

- Choose a beautiful notebook as your Tarot journal, one that delights you and feels special.

- Write your name inside its cover, set up the pages, and add your favorite images or colors. Make it yours!

- Decide: How will you use your Tarot journal? When? How often? Make it a personal commitment and stick to it. You'll be glad you did.

So, what are you waiting for? Start writing!

Section 1- Congratulations!

✔ You have a Tarot deck that's perfect for YOU.

✔ You've explored your Tarot deck, introduced yourself, and created a relationship with it.

✔ You've created a Tarot journal so you can keep track of your insights and personalised card meanings.

Now it's time to dive into the meanings of the Tarot cards themselves. Onward!

Section 2: Learn the Tarot Card Meanings (Days 6 to 21)

Learn how to interpret the 78 Tarot cards, using keywords, symbolism, numerology and stories.

Day 6: How to Learn the Tarot Card Meanings

Before we dive in, I want to take a moment to get a sense of your expectations. What do you think of when you picture yourself at the starting line of learning something new? Does it take you back to school, with endless repetition and reciting tables? Do you anticipate feeling frustrated, struggling with the learning curve that comes with being a newbie? Are you worried you might be "bad" at Tarot?

Well, I have good news: You don't have to worry about any of those things.

First, I'm not going to ask you to settle in for rote learning or memorization, not even for one second. Here's why:

For one thing, rote learning is, well, boring. I don't know about you, but I'd rather leave memorizing and cramming to my school days—not invite them into my passion hobby. And besides... that approach doesn't work! You could spend weeks, months, and even years, trying to commit the meanings of the cards to memory, only to sit down to a Tarot reading and find your mind has gone blank. I'm speaking from experience on this one! I took the memorization route in my early days of learning Tarot, and when I sat down to do a reading, I found I couldn't remember the meaning of a single card! Trying to cram that much information in your head is next to impossible unless you've got a super memory. But even that doesn't work because:

Rote learning shuts down your intuition. I see this happen all the time! One particular instance comes to mind, in which I was sitting in a local women's circle as each of us pored over our cards.

One of the ladies, Becky, had chosen the Empress. I could see her looking at this card with a big frown on her face. She looked puzzled, so I asked her what she saw in the card. But instead of dropping into her intuition, she said, "I don't know! I can't remember what this card means!" She was stressed out, and before I knew it, she was reaching for the book trying desperately to find out what the right meaning of the card was. It was such a missed opportunity!

You see, by putting her focus on getting it "right," Becky had ignored her intuition and missed out on the beautiful messages and insights waiting for her.

Now, don't get me wrong; it IS crucial that you are familiar with the traditional meanings of the cards—they are the essence of the Tarot, the ancient wisdom that we can tap into—but you shouldn't stop there. My goal is to show you how to use the Tarot cards to tap into your inner wisdom, where your intuitive self resides. Here is where the magic happens. And you need to put down the books and trust yourself if you want to connect with it (intuitive reading is also why it's impossible to be "bad" at Tarot!).

What is Intuition Anyway?

Intuition is your inner wisdom, that gut feeling or sense of knowing that feels like it resides deep within you. Those moments when you know something without really understanding how you know it? That's your intuition at work, bridging the gap between your conscious and unconscious mind. And I believe we all have intuition—it's not a "gift" bestowed on only a chosen few. The question is whether we choose to tap into this power (because that's exactly what it is!).

Your intuition frees you from other people's definitions and expectations. When you connect to your inner wisdom, you don't have to rely on others to tell you what to do.

Your intuition helps find flow and purpose in your life. As you move deeper into who you are, you will learn so much about what sparks your creative fire (and what puts it out).

Your intuition turns you into a creative powerhouse. By glimpsing the path of least resistance, you can manifest the goals that align with your highest good.

Your intuition tells you what you need to hear, not what you want to hear. When you can let go of your ego, you'll find it much easier to align your actions and intentions with the Universe.

And Tarot? Well, Tarot helps you hear what your intuitive Higher Self has to say. So, with that in mind, here are a few things I want you to know before we delve into my method for learning to read Tarot intuitively:

1. You can read the cards now—even if you're a total beginner. The learning curve is part of the process and, as you'll see in the chapters to come, is a valuable time to listen to your intuition.

2. There is no such thing as being "bad" at Tarot, just like there's no such thing as being "bad" at your intuition. You only need to say yes to your Higher Self and trust your inner wisdom.

3. Make it personal. The more you can connect the cards to your own stories and sense of the world, the better your reading will be. Pay close attention to how your experiences and life lessons talk to each card.

4. Be around people who support you and who can respect your journey toward being the best version of yourself. (That advice applies beyond just learning the Tarot, too.)

5. Your inner guidance is always available to you. Always. Sometimes the best thing you can do is sit quietly and ask it what it has to say.

6. More than anything, it's about balance.

If I could use only one word to describe the method I teach in this book, it would be *balance*. Put simply, learning the cards is about:

- Reading about what they mean
- Feeling into each card
- Learning to read the story in the card
- Knowing the systems (like numerology and the elements)
- Interpreting the symbolism in the card
- Attaching personal experiences to the cards to bring them to life

The traditional meanings of the cards will set a solid foundation of understanding, and the personal connections you make using your intuition will bring your readings to life. And with practice, those two sides, the traditional and the intuitive, will blend into a balanced Tarot practice that is 100% unique to you.

Be patient – this all happens over time. The important thing is that you start today (my job is to make sure you can do so with ease!) and that you see how the cards have many layers continually unfolding for you.

Activity

6.1 Create Your Own Keyword Charts

Over the next few l   essons about the Tarot Card Meanings, I'll be encouraging you to create your own Keyword Charts to support your learning process. Keywords are fantastic because they prompt your intuitive mind to kick into gear. One word might remind you of a feeling you had or an experience related to that card, and away you go.

On the flip-side, you can't do a reading with keywords only. It'd be a little weird and robotic. ("The Emperor. Structure and foundation. Oh, and High Priestess. Intuition.") So, use these wisely.

You can download my free keyword charts at **biddytarot.com/keywords-print**. You'll also get a free fillable keyword chart with your download. I encourage you to create your own keyword charts using this template.

If you're creating your own, here's what I recommend:

- Look at each card and connect with the energy of the card
- Brainstorm eight to ten different keywords or phrases that come to mind when you look at the card.
- Circle the two or three keywords that capture the essence of the card
- Add those to your keyword chart.

Simple as that!

(If you're very new to the Tarot, then you have my permission to throw in a bit of research to find out how others interpret the cards, BUT make sure you check in intuitively with the card too.)

Day 7: Learn About the Minor Arcana

OK, it's time to dive into the Tarot cards and their meanings!

Even though the deck leads with the Major Arcana cards, I like to begin with the Minor Arcana because they're easier to understand. The Major Arcana tend to represent those "big" energies in our lives. Their meanings are often more complex and nuanced, while the Minor Arcana relate to day-to-day situations, events, and even people. They're typically easier to understand because they mark the forces we interact with every day. So that's where we're going to start.

The Meanings of the Minor Arcana Tarot Cards

Don't be fooled! Even though the Minor Arcana are called "minor," it doesn't mean that these Tarot cards won't have a significant impact on your life. These cards reflect the trials and tribulations that you experience daily and can offer insight into how your present situation is affecting you and what steps you need to take to manifest your goals.

The Minor Arcana cards have a temporary influence—that is, they represent the energy moving through your life right now, which can be easily changed, depending on the actions you take.

The Minor Arcana Suits

There are four different Tarot Suits within the Minor Arcana:

- **The Suit of Cups** represents your feelings, emotions, intuition, and creativity. Cups cards often appear in Tarot readings about relationships and your emotional connection with yourself and others.

- **The Suit of Pentacles** represents your finances, work, and material possessions. Pentacles cards often appear in readings about career and financial wealth.

- **The Suit of Swords** represents your thoughts, words, and actions. Swords cards often appear in readings about communicating your ideas, making decisions, and asserting your power.

- **The Suit of Wands** represents your energy, motivation, and passion. The Wands cards often appear in readings about life purpose, spirituality, and new ideas.

Each Suit contains ten numbered cards and four Court cards (Page, Knight, Queen, and King). The Court cards each represent different personality characteristics we may express at any given time.

What Does a Minor Arcana Card Mean in a Tarot Reading?

In a Tarot reading, a Minor Arcana card will show you what's happening in your daily life— the interactions, experiences, thoughts, and emotions you encounter as you move through the world—and how it's affecting you. While a Major Arcana card will show you the critical life lesson you're learning, a Minor Arcana card will show you the situation you're dealing with currently. This situation is temporary and has the potential to change based on the actions you choose.

What Does it Mean When a Tarot Reading is Mostly Minor Arcana Tarot Cards?

When your Tarot reading has mostly Minor Arcana cards, it's a sign that you're dealing with day-to-day issues that will not necessarily have a lasting influence on your life. These issues are passing through, presenting you with an opportunity to learn from the experience. Look to any Major Arcana cards in the Tarot reading to identify and understand these lessons and how they may impact your life in the long-term.

The Four Elements

Mastering the elements, those ever-present forces in our universe, is a critical part of learning to read the Tarot. Once you connect to them deeply, you'll have a heightened awareness of how the Tarot Suits work, and your readings will be even more insightful.

Water, fire, earth, and air shape the Minor Arcana and lend a specific energy to each Suit.

When you combine the elements with numerology (from 1 to 10), which I'll teach you to do in the chapters to come, you'll unlock the meanings behind 40 of the 78 Tarot cards. Now that's an efficient way to learn Tarot!

The Four Elements

The four classical elements—water, fire, earth, and air—each carry their own energy and symbolic meaning:

- Water is feminine, symbolic of fluidity, feelings and emotions, intuition, relationships, healing, and cleansing. It corresponds to the Suit of Cups.

- Fire is masculine, symbolic of passion, energy, enthusiasm, and sexuality. It links to the Suit of Wands.

- Earth is feminine, grounded, stable, supportive, and fertile. The Suit of Pentacles is hers.

- Air is masculine and relates to knowledge, action, power, and change. The Suit of Swords is Air's domain.

Activity

7.1 Engage with the Elements

One of the most powerful ways to connect with the elements and understand their energy is to experience them firsthand. For example, experience the element of water by spending time at the beach or a nearby river. Watch the rainfall and the puddles form. Turn on the tap at home and feel the water run over your hands. Take a swim in the ocean.

Now it's your turn!

- Choose the Suit and element you want to work with.
- Observe the element in its purest form and watch how it expresses itself in different ways.
- Then, come back to your Tarot cards and look at how the element expresses itself in the cards.
- Pull out all the Cups cards, for example, and note the water in each card. What do you notice now? Is the water flowing or stagnant? Forceful or gentle? What new insights does this deepened understanding reveal to you?

Day 8: Learn About the Suit of Cups

The Suit of Cups deals with the emotional level of consciousness and associates with love, feelings, relationships, and connections. Its element is water, fluid, agile, and "in flow", and symbolic of feelings, intuition, healing, and cleansing; it can be gentle, like waves lapping against the sandy shore, but it's also forceful and formative, like a raging river. Its feminine energy reflects the subtle power that often dwells within women. The Suit of Cups is receptive, adaptable, purifying, and flowing.

What Do the Cups Tarot Cards Mean in a Reading?

Cups cards connect to creativity, romanticism, fantasy, and imagination. They suggest that you are thinking with your heart rather than your head and thus reflect your spontaneous responses and habitual reactions—those things you do without thinking. The negative aspects of the Suit of Cups include being overly emotional, disengaged or dispassionate, having unrealistic expectations, and fantasizing about what could be. Cups cards may also signify repressed emotions, an inability to express oneself, or a lack of creativity.

Generally, Cups people are emotional, artistic, humane, and creative. They hold a secure connection to their emotional selves and will draw energy from what they feel within. Cups Tarot cards often represent the "water" astrological signs: Pisces, Cancer, and Scorpio. When you see a Cups Court card in a reading, it usually relates to a person with a Pisces, Cancer, or Scorpio sun sign.

What Does it Mean When a Tarot Reading is Mostly Cups Tarot Cards?

Should a Tarot reading be predominantly Cups cards, you are seeking solutions to emotional conflicts, personal interactions, and matters of the heart, feelings, and creativity.

The Cards of the Suit of Cups

My hope is that you'll create your own connections with the Suit of Cups cards and their meanings. To help get you started, here are the core themes for each one:

Ace of Cups: New beginnings and opportunities in the realms of love, relationships, creative projects, and your emotional world. The seeds of potential have been planted. *What are they inviting you to explore or manifest?*

Two of Cups: Balance and reciprocation in deep partnerships and connections. A mutually beneficial union to be nurtured. The divine is present in everyone. *How are you recognizing and honoring it in your relationships?*

Three of Cups: Creative collaborations and group celebrations with friends and loved ones. You and your community can inspire each other to reach new heights. *How can you collaborate and celebrate?*

Four of Cups: Maintaining the current structure by saying no to new opportunities. A time of contemplation, meditation, and introspection before determining next steps. Your highest good is growing clearer. *What opportunities are in alignment, and what should you hold off on?*

Five of Cups: Conflicted emotions, feelings of regret, loss, and disappointment. Change is a constant in life. *What new opportunities has this loss cleared the way for?*

Six of Cups: Cooperation and harmony in relationships. Revisiting the innocent joy of childhood memories. An opportunity to start afresh from a positive place in relationships. *How can you open your heart to giving and receiving?*

Seven of Cups: An overwhelming variety of choices. Reflection and assessment are essential now to avoid falling prey to illusion and wishful thinking. You have a decision to make. *What do you need to know to choose wisely?*

Eight of Cups: Taking action to move on from a disappointing situation. You feel compelled to walk away, perhaps to escape. *What is no longer serving you, and what will bring you deeper fulfillment?*

Nine of Cups: Fulfillment and attainment on an emotional level. Your wishes have been fulfilled. *How can you feel sincere gratitude and share your abundance with others?*

Ten of Cups: A sense of completion and wholeness in your relationships. You have created blissful connections and emotional contentment by trusting your intuition. *How can you best appreciate everything you've accomplished?*

Page of Cups: An unexpected new idea, opportunity, or creative project. You may receive a pleasant surprise. There is a sense of possibility surrounding you. *What can you do to recognize and open yourself to new opportunities?*

Knight of Cups: Actively pursuing a creative project or romance, on a mission for peace and beauty. *Charm and romance abound. How can you give and receive love and harmony?*

Queen of Cups: A nurturing, intuitive mother figure, bringing compassion and emotional support. Your emotions are in balance. *How can you use your intuition and show loving-kindness to others?*

King of Cups: Mastery of emotions, creativity, and the unconscious mind. It's time to find a balance between your head and your heart. *How can you stay calm and in control of your emotions?*

To learn more about the individual card meanings of the Suit of Cups, please refer to The Ultimate Guide to Tarot Card Meanings. Find it at **biddytarot. com/ultimate-tarot**.

Activities

8.1 Journey Through the Suit of Cups

- Place all the Suit of Cups cards in front of you.
- Start by looking at each card and paying attention to the imagery and energy. What's happening in the card? Which symbols do you notice? What do you feel the card means? Can you get a sense of its lesson?
- Now, put the cards in order, from Ace to King, and examine their flow.

Can you see a story emerge?

- Pull out your Tarot journal and jot down the story you see as you move from one card to the next. How does it evolve?

- Use your journal to record any other insights, like recurring patterns, the mood or feel of the story, and any lessons that jump out to you.

8.2 Prepare a Suit of Cups Summary

Using the **Tarot Suit Summary Template** provided in the Appendix:

- Record the element associated with the Suit of Cups.

- Write down the keywords or key phrases you would associate with the Suit of Cups.

- List what you would see as this Suit's positive aspects and its negative or shadow aspects.

- List the types of day-to-day activities and events you would associate with this Suit.

- Identify the personality types and characteristics associated with the Suit of Cups.

- Collect images or pictures that you would associate with the Suit of Cups and create a "mood board" in your Tarot Journal.

Keep this Tarot Suit Summary on hand, or write it directly into your Tarot Journal.

8.3 Create Your Suit of Cups Keyword Chart

- Choose two to three keywords per card and add them to your Keyword Chart.

Day 9: Learn About the Suit of Pentacles

The Suit of Pentacles deals with the physical or external level of consciousness and thus mirrors the outer manifestations of your health, finances, work, and creativity. Pentacles cards speak to what we make of our external world—how we create it, shape it, transform it, and grow it. On a more esoteric level, Pentacles correlate with the ego, self-esteem, and self-image. Its element is earth, tactile and tangible, stable and supportive, the foundation from which the planet can grow and develop. Its feminine energy reflects the Earth's receptivity as it takes in nutrients and sunrays and then uses that energy to sustain the life that grows out of it. The Suit of Pentacles is grounded, stable, supportive, and fertile.

What Do the Pentacles Tarot Cards Mean in a Reading?

Pentacles cards speak to the material aspects of life, including work, business, property, money, and other material possessions. Their positive aspects include manifestation, realization, proof, and prosperity, while their negative aspects include being possessive, greedy and overly materialistic, over-indulgence and not exercising, mismanaging one's finances, and being career-focused to the detriment of other life priorities. The remedy to these negative aspects is often a return to nature to ground oneself and rediscover what is truly important.

Generally, Pentacles people are practical, career-minded, down-to-earth, and generous. They are tactile beings who like to experience the physical, tangible world in a sensory way. They are connected through the senses and seek pleasurable and sometimes indulgent experiences. Pentacles Tarot cards often represent the "earth" astrological signs: Taurus, Virgo, and Capricorn. When you see a Pentacles Court Card in a reading, it may relate to a person with a Taurus, Virgo, or Capricorn sun sign.

What Does it Mean When a Tarot Reading is Mostly Pentacles Tarot Cards?

Should a Tarot reading be predominantly Pentacles cards, you are seeking solutions to what are primarily material conflicts, financial matters, and concerns about your career and work.

The Cards of the Suit of Pentacles

My hope is that you'll create your own connections with the Suit of Pentacles cards and their meanings. To help get you started, here are the core themes for each one:

Ace of Pentacles: New beginnings and opportunities in business, career or finances. There is great potential for the manifestation of your material goals. *What action will you take to tap into this potential and achieve your ambitions?*

Two of Pentacles: Juggling a variety of priorities and responsibilities. You may need to be adaptable as your workload increases. *How are you managing your time and energy to maintain balance?*

Three of Pentacles: Collaborating with others will create the synergies needed to achieve big results. Detailed planning and working with a team or collective to get the job done. *Who can you collaborate with to achieve your goal, and how can you acknowledge their unique contribution?*

Four of Pentacles: An invitation to examine your relationship with money and material possessions. The possibility of a scarcity mindset, or attachment to possessions. *What are you clinging to, and how might you loosen your grip?*

Five of Pentacles: Feeling isolated due to financial loss and hard times in the realms of money, career and material possessions. A fear that you don't have "enough". *How can you redirect your attention to gratitude so that you can manifest what you desire?*

Six of Pentacles: Giving and receiving wealth, time and positive energy. Sharing from a place of generosity activates the harmonic flow of abundance. *How can you create a healthy exchange of energy with others?*

Seven of Pentacles: Investing time and energy into sustainable results and long-term rewards. Your hard work will pay off, be patient and stay the course. *Are you investing in the actions that will progress you towards your goals?*

Eight of Pentacles: Developing and mastering a skill through disciplined practice and hard work. Forging success through unwavering focus. *Where can you focus your attention to achieve mastery?*

Nine of Pentacles: Enjoying the abundance and luxury you have worked hard to create. Financial independence is achieved as the result of individual actions and efforts. *How can you appreciate the pleasures of the life you have created?*

Ten of Pentacles: A sense of accomplishment as you reach financial goals. You find joy in sharing your wealth and abundance with loved ones. *How are you creating a lasting foundation for a sustainable future?*

Page of Pentacles: New beginnings and inspiration for projects in your material life. The possibility of studying towards a new job or career. You can create whatever you want with focused intention and action. *What are you focusing on to turn your dreams into reality?*

Knight of Pentacles: Working methodically towards your goals. Routine, repetition and sticking to the plan will ensure you see success. *How can you establish a routine and dedicate your efforts to achieve your vision?*

Queen of Pentacles: Maintaining a healthy balance between home and work. Nurturing yourself and others to create a calm and harmonious life. Being practical and resourceful leads to abundance. *How are you creating a healthy balance between all of the responsibilities in your life?*

King of Pentacles: Confidence and mastery in attracting and managing wealth. The ultimate business owner and leader, providing guidance and wisdom in business and finance. *How are you attracting and maintaining prosperity in your life?*

To learn more about the individual card meanings of the Suit of Pentacles, please refer to The Ultimate Guide to Tarot Card Meanings at **biddytarot. com/ultimate-tarot**.

Activities

9.1 Journey Through the Suit of Pentacles

- Place all the Suit of Pentacles cards in front of you.

- Start by looking at each card and paying attention to the imagery and energy. What's happening in the card? Which symbols do you notice? What do you feel the card means? Can you get a sense of its lesson?

- Now, put the cards in order, from Ace to King, and examine their flow. Can you see a story emerge?

- Pull out your Tarot journal and jot down the story you see as you move from one card to the next. How does it evolve?

- Use your journal to record any other insights, like recurring patterns, the mood or feel of the story, and any lessons that jump out to you.

9.2 Prepare a Suit of Pentacles Summary

Using the **Tarot Suit Summary Template** provided in the Appendix:

- Record the element associated with the Suit of Pentacles.

- Write down the keywords or key phrases you would associate with the Suit of Pentacles.

- List what you would see as this Suit's positive aspects and its negative or shadow aspects.

- List the types of day-to-day activities and events you would associate with this Suit.

- Identify the personality types and characteristics associated with the Suit of Pentacles.

- Collect images or pictures that you would associate with the Suit of Pentacles and create a "mood board" in your Tarot Journal.

Keep this Tarot Suit Summary on hand, or write it directly into your Tarot Journal.

9.3 Create Your Suit of Pentacles Keyword Chart

- Choose two to three keywords per card and add them to your Keyword Chart.

Day 10: Learn About the Suit of Swords

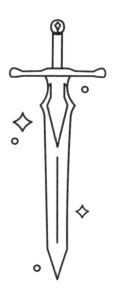

The Suit of Swords deals with the mental level of consciousness, centered on the mind and the intellect. Swords cards mirror the quality of mind present in your thoughts, attitudes, and beliefs. They are often double-edged and, in this way, symbolize the delicate balance between intellect and power. As such, Swords must be balanced by spirit (Wands) and feeling (Cups) to have the most positive effect. Given its malleability, is it any wonder that the Suit of Swords corresponds to air—intangible and unseen, but also in constant movement? Air can be still and unnoticed, or it can be a breeze or a fierce wind. It is mighty, yet refreshing and cleansing. Its masculine energy is capable of leading by force and power, even though it remains unseen. Symbolically, the Suit of Swords relates to knowledge, action, power, and change.

What Do the Swords Tarot Cards Mean in a Reading?

The Suit of Swords associates with action, change, force, power, oppression, ambition, courage, and conflict. But remember: action can be constructive *and* destructive. The Swords cards' negative aspects include anger, guilt, harsh judgment, a lack of compassion, and verbal and mental abuse.

Generally, Swords people are intelligent, thoughtful, logical, and excellent communicators. They are rational beings and like to experience the world by understanding and analyzing the happenings around them. But Swords people can also be ruthless, domineering, confrontational, and rigid. Swords Tarot cards often represent the "air" astrological signs: Aquarius, Libra, and Gemini. When you see a Swords Court Card in a reading, it often relates to a person with an Aquarius, Libra, or Gemini sun sign.

What Does it Mean When a Tarot Reading is Mostly Swords Tarot Cards?

Should a Tarot reading be predominantly Swords cards, you are seeking solutions to what are primarily mental struggles: conflict, arguments, and decisions that must be made. There could even be violence present. While Swords can carry with them many negative or forceful messages, they also serve as a warning to be more cautious of what is occurring around you.

The Cards of the Suit of Swords

My hope is that you'll create your own connections with the Suit of Swords cards and their meanings. To help get you started, here are the core themes for each one:

Ace of Swords: A new idea or new way of thinking paves the way for a break-through. New opportunities and inspiration that draw upon your creative and intellectual abilities. *How can you expand your mind and perspective?*

Two of Swords: Needing to make a challenging decision may result in no decision or action at all. To avoid a stalemate, use both your head and your heart to weigh up the options. *How can you open your eyes to the possibilities?*

Three of Swords: Feelings of deep emotional pain and disappointment. A reminder that the discomfort of hardship helps you grow. *How can you see the pain and challenges as a learning opportunity and rise stronger than ever?*

Four of Swords: A period of rest and reflection in solitude. Replenish your mental, emotional and physical strength before taking on the next challenge. *How can you create time and space to rest and reevaluate your priorities?*

Five of Swords: A sense of defeat and loss after a conflict. Choosing your battles wisely will lead to more peace than engaging in every disagreement. *How can you collaborate, instead of compete?*

Six of Swords: A period of transition as you leave behind the familiar and step into the unknown. Making a mental shift for your personal growth. *What baggage can you release in order to move forward?*

Seven of Swords: Escaping a responsibility or commitment, possibly with deception and betrayal in order to get away with something. Be strategic in what you do and how you prioritize your responsibilities, as well as in who you trust. *Where do you need to be more honest and authentic in your life?*

Eight of Swords: Limiting beliefs are no longer serving you. A victim mentality is holding you back, making you feel trapped and unable to see solutions. *How can you reclaim your power and set yourself free?*

Nine of Swords: Excessive worry and negative thoughts are leaving you stressed and anxious. Potential insomnia or nightmares as your constant, negative thoughts prevent you from resting. *Who can you reach out to for help in seeing things differently and finding a solution?*

Ten of Swords: A painful and unexpected ending, possibly involving betrayal. The final ordeal before brighter days. *What wisdom can you gain from this hurt and defeat?*

Page of Swords: Exploring a new way of thinking, learning or communicating. Energy, passion and enthusiasm around a new project. *What new forms of expression are available to you?*

Knight of Swords: Ambition and motivation to succeed lead to swift action and a determination to make things happen. Use the power of your intellect to achieve your goals. *What energizes you to take action?*

Queen of Swords: Intellectual maturity and mental clarity allow unbiased judgments. Upfront and honest in your views, as a truth-seeker, you expect the same from others. *How can you gain the information you need to make the best decisions?*

King of Swords: Standing firm in your truth and expressing yourself with authority and intellectual power. An impartial, professional advisor and guide. *How can you remain impartial in making important decisions?*

To learn more about the individual card meanings of the Suit of Swords, please refer to The Ultimate Guide to Tarot Card Meanings at **biddytarot. com/ultimate-tarot**.

Activities

10.1 Journey Through the Suit of Swords

- Place all the Suit of Swords cards in front of you.
- Start by looking at each card and paying attention to the imagery and energy. What's happening in the card? Which symbols do you notice? What do you feel the card means? Can you get a sense of its lesson?
- Now, put the cards in order, from Ace to King, and examine their flow. Can you see a story emerge?
- Pull out your Tarot journal and jot down the story you see as you move from one card to the next. How does it evolve?
- Use your journal to record any other insights, like recurring patterns, the mood or feel of the story, and any lessons that jump out to you.

10.2 Prepare a Suit of Swords Summary

Using the **Tarot Suit Summary Template** provided in the Appendix:

- Record the element associated with the Suit of Swords.
- Write down the keywords or key phrases you would associate with the Suit of Swords.
- List what you would see as this Suit's positive aspects and its negative or shadow aspects.
- List the types of day-to-day activities and events you would associate with this Suit.
- Identify the personality types and characteristics associated with the Suit of Swords.
- Collect images or pictures that you would associate with the Suit of Swords and create a "mood board" in your Tarot Journal.

Keep this Tarot Suit Summary on hand, or write it directly into your Tarot Journal.

10.3 Create Your Suit of Swords Keyword Chart

- Choose two to three keywords per card and add them to your Keyword Chart.

Day 11: Learn About the Suit of Wands

The Suit of Wands is imbued with primal energy, the seeds through which life springs forth: spirituality, inspiration, determination, strength, intuition, creativity, ambition and expansion, and original thought. Its element is fire, hot, wild, unpredictable, and energetic; it can be creative, in helping us to cook food or build tools, or it can be destructive, like a devastating bushfire or a house fire. Its masculine energy reflects drive and willpower. The Suit of Wands is passionate, energized, enthusiastic, and sexual.

What Do the Wands Tarot Cards Mean in a Reading?

The Wands cards deal with the spiritual level of consciousness and mirror what is important to you at the core of your being. They address what makes you tick—your personality, ego, enthusiasm, self-concept, and personal energy, both internal and external. Their negative aspects include illusion, egotistical behavior, impulsiveness, a lack of direction or purpose, or feeling meaningless.

Generally, Wands people are energetic, charismatic, warm, and spiritual. Wands Tarot cards often represent the "fire" astrological signs: Leo, Sagittarius, and Aries. When you see a Wands Court Card in a reading, it often relates to a person with a Leo, Sagittarius, or Aries sun sign.

What Does it Mean When a Tarot Reading is Mostly Wands Tarot Cards?

Should a Tarot reading be predominantly Wands cards, you are seeking solutions to issues in the realm of thought or that are in the early stages of development. You may also be seeking a higher purpose and meaning in your life and want to understand more about what motivates and energizes you.

The Cards of the Suit of Wands

My hope is that you'll create your own connections with the Suit of Wands cards and their meanings. To help get you started, here are the core themes for each one:

Ace of Wands: Pure potential in the spiritual and energetic realms. Flowing ideas that inspire you to follow a new path. *How can you follow your heart and live your passion?*

Two of Wands: Exploring your options and creating an action plan for the future. Discovering what's possible when you step out of your comfort zone. *How can you use your intuition to confirm your plan of action?*

Three of Wands: Dream bigger than your limitations as you expand and grow. Take the next step towards your vision and broaden your horizons. *What can you create with the new opportunities available to you?*

Four of Wands: Joyful celebration with loved ones. Feeling supported and secure in a home environment. *Who can you surround yourself with to enjoy happiness and stability?*

Five of Wands: Differences of opinions can lead to conflict and tension. Everyone is fighting to be heard, so take the time to listen. *How can you direct the energy of the group for ideal outcomes?*

Six of Wands: Confidence and self-assurance after achieving a significant goal. A public win or recognition gives you the strength to continue your endeavors. *How can you have faith in yourself and what you have accomplished?*

Seven of Wands: External challenges may stand in the way of you pursuing your goals. Having to protect what you've achieved and earned from competitors who want to take your place. *What do you stand for, and how can you draw on your self-belief to protect it?*

Eight of Wands: Forward momentum to manifest your goals. An enthusiastic busy period where fast action produces significant results. *Where can you focus your energy to pursue the best options available?*

Nine of Wands: Resilience and perseverance through the challenges on your path. You will reach your goal and eventually prosper if you maintain your position. *How can you establish firm boundaries to protect your energy?*

Ten of Wands: Taking on extra responsibility may lead to exhaustion. You've been working hard towards a goal, and the end is in sight. *How can you manage your time in order to free yourself up for rest when you need it?*

Page of Wands: Exploring ideas for a new creative venture. Test your ideas and map out a plan to make the creative spark a reality. *What could you create if you had no limitations?*

Knight of Wands: Channeling your energy for a mission into inspired action. Bold and courageous pursuit of your vision and purpose. *Do your ideas and actions align with your goals?*

Queen of Wands: You have the confidence to stand in your power and shine your light. Inspiring others with your vibrancy, you are masterful at engaging others to help you achieve your goals. *How can you fully express yourself and your passions?*

King of Wands: A visionary, charismatic leader. You will achieve your dreams when you live your life with intent, vision and a long-term view. *How can you be mindful in your intentions to create the outcome you want?*

To learn more about the individual card meanings of the Suit of Wands, please refer to The Ultimate Guide to Tarot Card Meanings at **biddytarot. com/ultimate-tarot**.

Activities

11.1 Journey Through the Suit of Wands

- Place all the Suit of Wands cards in front of you.

- Start by looking at each card and paying attention to the imagery and energy. What's happening in the card? Which symbols do you notice? What do you feel the card means? Can you get a sense of its lesson?

- Now, put the cards in order, from Ace to King, and examine their flow. Can you see a story emerge?

- Pull out your Tarot journal and jot down the story you see as you move from one card to the next. How does it evolve?

- Use your journal to record any other insights, like recurring patterns, the mood or feel of the story, and any lessons that jump out to you.

11.2 Prepare a Suit of Wands Summary

Using the **Tarot Suit Summary Template** provided in the Appendix:

- Record the element associated with the Suit of Wands.

- Write down the keywords or key phrases you would associate with the Suit of Wands.

- List what you would see as this Suit's positive aspects and its negative or shadow aspects.

- List the types of day-to-day activities and events you would associate with this Suit.

- Identify the personality types and characteristics associated with the Suit of Wands.

- Collect images or pictures that you would associate with the Suit of Wands and create a "mood board" in your Tarot Journal.

Keep this Tarot Suit Summary on hand, or write it directly into your Tarot Journal.

11.3 Create Your Suit of Wands Keyword Chart

- Choose two to three keywords per card and add them to your Keyword Chart.

Day 12: Learn About the Court Cards

What do I do with the court cards? It's one of the biggest challenges in learning to read Tarot and a question I get asked all the time. Is the court card a person? And if so, who is it? Is it you or someone else? And if it's not a person, what else can it be? A situation? An event? *Argh!* See how confusing it can be!?

No wonder hundreds of people who are learning Tarot come to me saying, "Brigit, I've got no idea with these court cards. Help me interpret them!" So, in today's lesson, I want to introduce you to the Court Cards and share with you one of the easiest ways you can interpret their appearance in your Tarot readings.

About the Court Cards

The sixteen Court Cards are part of the Minor Arcana, and there are four members of the Court within each Suit—the Page, Knight, Queen, and King. The Court Cards blend the characteristics of the Page, Knight, Queen, or King with the characteristics of the assigned Suit. Before we dig into how to interpret the Court Cards, let me introduce you to the different members of the Court and what each represents.

Pages

Pages represent the start of a journey or a new project. For example, the Page of Cups may speak of a new creative project, or the Page of Pentacles may relate to starting a new course. Pages also represent a time where we are expressing a new aspect of ourselves. For example, the Page of Swords may show you're expressing yourself in new ways, through verbal or written communication. You certainly haven't mastered the art of communication in the way the King of Swords might have, but you are at the very beginning of this journey as you explore how you can express this new idea or thought.

Pages have a beautiful, *fresh* energy. They are still developing a sense of self, but they approach new challenges with fervent energy and excitement. Pages look forward to the opportunity to learn and practice new skills.

On a physical level, Pages can represent young children through young adults. However, don't limit yourself by thinking a Page can only represent someone under 30. Pages can also represent those who are young at heart or who are discovering a new aspect of themselves.

I once had a client in her 60s who asked about changing jobs and moving to a new university. The Page of Wands appeared in her reading, and I saw it as a clear sign that the move would enable her to develop her skills in a new area of expertise and to reignite her passion for her work. As it turned out, this new opportunity meant that she could work on a new project outside her usual area of expertise. So, she was embracing the energy of the Page, even though she wasn't as young as the traditional Page.

As situations or events, Pages are often seen as messengers and come to you with a new opportunity or an invitation. They often appear when you are on the cusp of a new idea (Wands), a new feeling (Cups), a new way of thinking (Swords) or a new job or career pursuit (Pentacles)—and they can even symbolize a new stage in life. Pages encourage you to go for it and give you the green light for a new project or initiative.

Knights

The Knights are like crusaders—mission-focused, highly action-oriented (more so than Pages), and dedicated to making things happen. The Knight's journey is already underway, and he is intent on keeping that journey going, no matter what.

That's the thing about the Knights. They have enough experience under their belt to know what they're doing, but what they do not have is the full life experience that the King and Queen possess. Knights are prone to taking things to an extreme and such excessive feelings and behavior are not always a good thing.

For example, the Knight of Swords has an excess of ambition. Once he has his mind fixed on a goal, he will do anything and everything to achieve it. There's nothing inherently wrong with that, but the downside is that he may rush into things and railroad others to get what he wants. He doesn't have the King of Swords' maturity to take a moderate approach, and thus, the Knight of Swords can end up charging down the wrong path if he's not careful.

Always consider both sides of a Knight—does he represent a helpful or harmful approach? What is in excess and where could you use a bit of moderation? Or, conversely, where could you use a little more excess?

The Knight of Pentacles is a good example of what I mean. On the one hand, he is steady, dependable, and hardworking. But he can be dull and "routine" too. It also comes down to what situations or relationships he finds himself in. If he is working in a hierarchical firm, then he's a perfect fit. But he may not be as successful in a creative advertising agency.

On a physical level, Knights can represent adults between 20 and 35 (more or less). Remember, though, not to be limited by this suggested age bracket.

As events or situations, Knights reflect movement, change, and action. They are always on the move, looking for the next big opportunity and encourage you to do the same!

Queens

Now we move into the "mature" Court cards. The four Queens and the four Kings have attained a level of personal development and mastery where they can take a more balanced, even-tempered approach.

The difference between the Queens and the Kings is that the Queens are in a state of receptivity and openness, whereas the Kings have attained what they believe is complete mastery and are focused on putting their knowledge out into the world. It's between these two members of the Court that we see the balance of the feminine and masculine energies shine through.

Now, don't get locked into thinking Queens can only represent women. The Queens also represent feminine energy—opening, receiving, relating, surrendering, being and nurturing—and this energy is available to both women and men. They tap into the feminine energy of nurturing and caring for others, and give way to creating a more sustainable approach to life. A Queen provides nourishment and sustenance that will keep her ideas and actions going.

Queens typically express their Suits from the inside. They have mastered the power of gentle persuasion, setting the tone without imposing their point of view. It reminds me of the saying, "Behind every great man is a great woman." She gently and subtly influences, without being seen as pushy or domineering. In this way, we can view Queens as the most powerful because they influence with no one realizing.

One of my Tarot reading clients was going through a divorce and wanted to know how she could best support her son through the process. When the Queen of Wands came up in her reading, it stood out to me that she needed to provide positive energy to her son, supporting him and keeping optimistic even while she was dealing with some very trying times. It wasn't that she needed to lie and pretend everything was OK, but she needed to protect him from the negativity that crops up during the divorce process. The Queen of Wands' message resonated for her and gave her a path forward.

On a physical level, Queens often represent people aged between 30 and 50 who have a good amount of life experience under their belt.

As events or situations, Queens represent creativity and ideas coming to fruition. Queens are also very feminine and nurturing cards, reflecting the rites of passage for women, from embracing sexuality to motherhood to caring for others.

Kings

The Kings represent mastery. They have traveled through life successfully and are now at the pinnacle of experience and understanding. Thus, the Kings represent the developed personalities of each Suit. Kings cards embody masculine energy—penetrating, leading, doing, striving, and asserting— but, as with the Queens, they are not limited to simply representing men in a Tarot reading. They represent the masculine energy within all human beings.

As people, Kings have full control over their feelings, emotions, thoughts, and actions. They are reliable, solid, and can direct the flow of their energy to achieve their visions and goals. Kings like to be seen as the providers, taking responsibility for others' well-being. They want to make a difference and impact the world, drawing upon the various elements of their personalities to make their mark.

On a physical level, Kings often represent older males aged 40 and above and those in leadership roles.

Pages conceive ideas; Knights act upon ideas, Queens nurture ideas, and now Kings develop those ideas to an established and stable state. Thus, as an event or situation, Kings signify the growth and maturity of an idea or concept right through to completion.

Court Cards in a Reading

OK, here comes the tricky bit. What does a Court Card mean in a Tarot reading!?

Well, here's my motto when it comes to learning Tarot: KISS (Keep It Simple, Seeker)!

If we are going to keep things super simple (and I recommend that you do if you're beginning to learn how to read Tarot), then see the court cards as an aspect of your personality.

See the court cards as an aspect of your personality

We know the Tarot deck has 16 court cards, and I believe that each one of us has a little (or a lot) of each court card within us. At different times and in different situations with different people and different interactions, we will express different parts of our personality.

For example, when you're having a fun, playful time with your kids, then your Page of Cups comes out. But when your kids complain about cutting their toast in triangles instead of squares, maybe your Queen of Swords reversed starts to come out. Or maybe when you're with your husband, you're a total Queen of Wands. Or, you're out with a long-time friend, someone you've known for many, many years, so you get a bit more mischievous, and your Knight of Wands comes out.

You're still the same person; you just express these different aspects of yourself in different situations. And so, if we think of the court cards as facets of our own personality, we see that we can express a court card in different times and different scenarios.

I encourage you to keep it simple while you're in early stages of your Tarot exploration (hello, Page energy!), but when you feel ready, you can expand your perspective of the court cards.

Is the Court Card Me or Someone Else?

When you decide to widen your scope on the court cards, the next question is typically: "Does this card represent an actual person? Is it me, or is it somebody else? If it's somebody else, then *who on earth is it?*" This is where things can get complicated, but guess what—my advice is the same. Keep it simple, seeker! Set the intention that every time you do a Tarot reading, a court card will represent you.

See the court cards as you first

Let's say you ask, "What do I need to do to find my next job?" and get the Page of Wands. Now, without a clear intention, you might think, "Page of Wands? Is this me, or is it someone else? Is this someone who is going to get the job? Maybe the person who'll interview me? Or my future boss? What is this card?"

But, in your new way of reading Tarot, where you're keeping things simple and setting your intention, you know that whenever a court card shows up, it's going to be about you. So, in this case, you know the Page of Wands is a part of your personality that you need to express to find your next job. Nice and simple, right?

Let's be crystal clear: A court card will represent you unless its position states that it represents someone else. So, if you were doing a Celtic Cross spread, for example, and a court card turns up in the External Influences position, it will not be about you. It's about somebody else.

And to find out who that somebody else is, you need to ask yourself, "Who in my life right now is expressing themselves as the Queen of Swords?" (or whichever court card appears in your reading). Keep in mind that you're not asking, "Who *is* the Queen of Swords?" This person may just be interacting with you in that way right now, but you may find later that she's acting more like a Queen of Cups or Page of Pentacles. Minor Arcana cards can always change.

As you become more confident and experienced with your Tarot readings, you won't have to stick to the rule that a court card will always represent you (or the person asking the question). I find when I'm doing a Tarot reading and see a court card, I relate it to myself or whoever I'm reading for first, but now and then my intuition might kick in and say, "I'm not sure it's me. I think it might be someone else or something else." I can be more flexible, but that's because I'm comfortable and confident with the court cards.

You'll feel like that soon—trust me. If you don't feel like that now, it's coming. It really is. But for now, to help you get really confident, just stick to that nice keep-it-simple rule, and treat a court card as a representation of you and the facet of your personality you're expressing.

What Else Might a Court Card Represent?

So, we know that a Court Card often relates to an aspect of ourselves that is being expressed in a specific situation. But, sometimes, a Court card may also allude to a situation or its "personality." For example, the Page of Cups often signals an invitation or an offer that brings a lot of joy and excitement. Or the King of Wands suggests a situation where you are maturing your goals and visions in life.

Court cards can also represent situations where the client is bringing part of their own personality to that situation. Let's say the Queen of Wands appears in relation to, "What is happening at work?" We know the Queen of Wands is a sociable and outgoing personality, and so it's likely that your client is bringing this energy to work, creating a situation conducive to networking and building new relationships.

Or, let's say the Page of Swords appears in a reading about a new relationship. We know this Page is a curious and eager young fellow, so it is likely that, again, the client is bringing this energy to the relationship. In this way, too, the "personality" of the relationship is that new, energetic phase where each person is getting to know the other, and every interaction has that delicious fluttery energy.

OK, I want to check in with you: how are you doing over there? Is your head full with all the possibilities of Court Cards? Or is there room for a little more? If your cup is full, then come back to this section later. But if you're open to learning one more technique for interpreting Court Cards, then read on.

Elemental Associations of the Court Cards

Just as the four Suits of the Minor Arcana associate with the elements, so, too, do the four court card types. Their elemental associations can be a very helpful way to break down the court cards and tap into their true essence. Here's the breakdown:

- Page — Air (intellectual, sensible, logical, clear-sighted)
- Knight — Fire (passionate, active, courageous, energetic)

- Queen — Water (emotional, intuitive, sensitive)
- King — Earth (practical, down-to-earth, materialistic)

Thus, each Court Card has a dual elemental association—one element associated with the court card itself and one element associated with the Suit (see the table below).

Suit	Page (Air)	Knight (Fire)	Queen (Water)	King (Earth)
Cups (Water)	Air/Water	Fire/Water	Water/Water	Earth/Water
Pentacles (Earth)	Air/Earth	Fire/Earth	Water/Earth	Earth/Earth
Swords (Air)	Air/Air	Fire/Air	Water/Air	Earth/Air
Wands (Fire)	Air/Fire	Fire/Fire	Water/Fire	Earth/Fire

Knowing the elemental associations adds another layer to your interpretations of the Court Cards. For example, the Page of Wands represents a combination of Air (Page) and Fire (Wands), someone who is action-oriented and driven by ideas.

And for court cards with two of the same element, think of them as "double-strength." The Page of Swords, for example, has a two-times strong connection with Air. Therefore, this card is intellectual, curious, and clear-sighted.

Court Cards that have complementary elemental associations (Fire/Air and Earth/Water) take a balanced approach to life and are well-rounded, flexible, and adaptable. The King of Cups, for example, balances his head and heart perfectly. He is the master of his inner and outer worlds as he has control of his emotions.

Court Cards with opposing elements (Fire/Water and Earth/Air) are often polarized individuals with dual personalities and shadow selves. They can be unpredictable, but this isn't always a bad thing. The Knight of Cups, for example, is romantic and charming, but he is also prone to fantasy or bouts of moodiness. Other combinations, like Fire/Earth and Air/Water have little effect on each other and are considered neutral.

Note that these elemental associations work not only in the Court cards but also in Tarot readings where there is an interaction between elements.

Activities

12.1 Which Court Card Are You?

- Think about how you relate with different people in your life and pick a Court Card that represents you in those situations. For example, when I'm on a live training with thousands of people watching worldwide, I am channeling my inner Queen of Wands. And when I'm at home on the weekend, creating a new macramé wall-hanging, I'm the Page of Cups.

- If you come up with a few particularly resonant expressions, note them down in your Tarot journal.

12.2 Develop Court Card Profiles

- For each Court Card, write your thoughts on each of the following:
- Character strengths
- Character weaknesses
- Personal mantra
- Possible career and/or life path (or paths)
- Associated situations

For example, here's what I might write for the Page of Pentacles:

- Character strengths—practical and well-planned
- Character weaknesses—conservative and risk-averse
- Personal mantra/advice—manifest your dreams
- Possible career/life paths—a small business owner, an accountant, a business graduate, a lifelong student
- Associated situations—starting a new job, turning an idea into a project

Keep your profiles in your Tarot journal. They will come in handy as you keep working with the court cards.

12.3 Go Speed Dating with the Court Cards

Imagine. It's Thursday night, and you're heading down to your local hangout. As you open the door, you hear a buzz of activity and see sixteen people eagerly chatting away. It's speed-dating night for the court cards!

- Select two court cards
- Imagine these two characters sitting at a table together, with five minutes to get to know each other. What do they look like? What do they say to each other? How's their chemistry? Is it a match made in heaven? Or a complete turnoff?
- Record your insights in your Tarot journal

Go on, have some fun with it!

Day 13: Learn About the Major Arcana

You've explored the 56 cards of the Minor Arcana. Now let's dive into the 22 Major Arcana cards!

The Meanings of the Major Arcana Tarot Cards

The Major Arcana Tarot cards represent the life lessons, karmic influences, and the big archetypal themes influencing your life and your soul's journey to enlightenment. The Major Arcana card meanings are rich and complex in beautiful ways! These Tarot cards truly represent the structure of human consciousness and hold the keys to life lessons passed down through the ages.

The Major Arcana includes 21 numbered cards and one unnumbered card (the Fool). Think of the Fool as the main character of the Major Arcana. He makes his journey through each of the cards, meeting new teachers and learning new life lessons along the way, and reaches the culmination of his journey with the World card. This progression is known as the "Fool's Journey" and is a helpful way of understanding the storyline of the Major Arcana card meanings.

The Major Arcana cards can also represent Carl Jung's archetypes—the consistent, directing patterns of influence that are an inherent part of the collective unconscious and human nature. Their themes mark, portray, and symbolize stages in our psyche, whereby we aim to become balanced and integrated individuals. Along this journey, we encounter challenges, face adversity, make difficult decisions, and fight opposing forces. Each step of the way brings us closer to enlightenment. In that way, we are not so different from the Fool.

Life Lessons and the Fool's Journey

Let's explore the Fool's journey further. It's a powerful way to understand the lessons of the Major Arcana cards.

In this journey, we begin with the *Fool*—the unnumbered card. The Fool is the "child," a blank slate, ready to embrace the world and everything it has to offer. He has no fear because he hasn't experienced enough to know what ought to scare him.

The first person the Fool meets along the way is the *Magician*, who shows him that as long as he can stay grounded and connect with the Source, he will be able to manifest whatever he wants.

The Fool moves on to the *High Priestess*, who builds on what the Magician has taught him and shows the Fool that the world isn't always what it seems and, in fact, there is a more profound mystery to the world. She shows the Fool the underworld and that which cannot be seen.

Next, the Fool encounters the *Empress,* the mother figure, who shows him love and nurturing. The *Emperor* follows with his rules and structure. The *Hierophant* teaches the Fool how to think and behave and what to believe. And by the time he reaches the *Lovers*, the Fool realizes that he is now on his own and can make choices for himself.

The *Chariot* shows him that when he sets his mind to something, he can move forward. And *Strength* reminds him that he doesn't always have to be striving like the Chariot, but he can find his power and strength from within, without force. He then meets the *Hermit*, a wise, old soul who has found his path by traveling alone. The Fool realizes that his answers lie within and spending time in isolation will help him connect with those answers.

Next, the Fool encounters the *Wheel of Fortune* and discovers that life is full of ups and downs, and sometimes he must ride the wave. And just as he hands his life over to destiny and fate, *Justice* steps in to remind him that he has choices and his actions will carry consequences, both positive and negative. By the time the Fool reaches the *Hanged Man*, he realizes that sometimes he needs to surrender and look at the world from a different perspective.

Death shows the Fool that nothing lasts forever and we are in a constant state of change. Metaphorical "death" is imminent and allows for a transition into another stage of life.

The Fool then meets *Temperance* and discovers that balance, harmony, and moderation is the way to a good life... That is until the *Devil* steps in and demonstrates to the Fool that without balance, addiction and obsession can occur. The Devil has a hold on the Fool, luring him in with temptation until the *Tower* upends his world and everything the Fool thought was "true" and finite comes crashing down. It's time for a re-evaluation. With destruction comes the opportunity for creation.

And now the Fool meets the *Star*, filled with transformation, hope, and faith. The Fool has traversed the dark night of the soul and is seeing the light once again. When he meets with the *Moon*, he is reminded that not everything is what it seems and he is drawn to his subconscious mind where shadows lurk, and fears remain.

Next, he meets with the *Sun* and is filled with renewed energy, knowing that life is abundant and that he is blessed. As the Fool encounters *Judgment*, he is reborn. He is a new person, with a new perspective on life, having traveled this soul path.

And finally, he reaches the *World*, and his journey is complete—or is it? He steps through the wreath with the dancing woman and finds himself back at the beginning again.

This is the beauty of Tarot! It shows us this progression through life and introduces us to the path of spiritual self-awareness and the various stages we encounter as we search for greater significance and understanding. To say the Major Arcana cards hold meaningful lessons is a huge understatement. They encapsulate the flows and rhythms of life itself!

What Does a Major Arcana Card Mean in a Tarot Reading?

When you see a Major Arcana card in a Tarot reading, you are being called to reflect on the life lessons and themes you're experiencing. A Major Arcana card will often set the scene for the entire Tarot reading, with the other cards relating back to that core Major Arcana meaning. You can also look to the Minor Arcana cards in the reading to understand how this life lesson or theme is playing out in your daily life. For example, the Chariot with the Four of Swords might imply a disconnect between what you know you need to do (push forward) versus what you are doing (resting and relaxing).

What Does it Mean When a Tarot Reading is Mostly Major Arcana Tarot Cards?

When a Tarot reading is predominantly made up of Major Arcana cards, you are experiencing life-changing events that will have long-term effects. The experience carries important lessons that you must pay attention to in order to progress further in your spiritual and personal quest.

If most of the Major Arcana Tarot cards are reversed, however, it may be a sign that you are not paying enough attention to these important life lessons and you need to first master the lesson before being able to move forward. For example, one client had the Death card reversed show up in her reading about moving overseas. Her husband had recently received a promotion that required them to move to another country, but she was resisting the change. Seeing the Death card reversed in the reading, she realized that she was being shown how to embrace "death" and change, and this move was an opportunity for her to develop personally.

Embodying the Energy of the Major Arcana Cards

The beautiful thing about the Major Arcana is that you can embody the energy of these cards and use it to create positive change and transformation. Here is a great opportunity to be more proactive with the cards and make a little magic happen! For example, if you want to connect with the intuitive energy of the High Priestess, get to know the card and explore it on a personal level, and you'll find that its energy manifests in your life. (I'll show you a neat technique later that involves meditating with the cards—it's super powerful!)

Activities

13.1 Get to Know the Major Arcana

- Place all the Major Arcana cards in front of you.

- Start by looking at each card and paying attention to the imagery and energy. What's happening in the card? What symbols do you notice? What do you feel the card means? What's the lesson of the card?

- Record your insights in your Tarot journal.

13.2 Create Your Own Fool's Journey

- Place the Major Arcana cards in order, starting with the Fool and ending with the World.

- In your Tarot journal, write the journey of the Fool as he meets each "teacher." What life lesson does each card share with the Fool? And how does it build on the previous lesson learned? Do you see any patterns as you move through this exercise?

- And for bonus points, where are you on this journey? What life lessons are you learning?

13.3. Create a Major Arcana Keyword Chart

- Now that you've explored the Major Arcana, choose two to three keywords per card and add them to your Keyword Chart. You can download a fillable keyword chart at **biddytarot.com/keywords-print**.

Day 14: Learn Tarot by Numbers

Want to know the secret to learning the Tarot card meanings quickly? Learn the meanings of the numbers from 1 to 10. It will give you a huge head start in your readings. You see, Tarot and numerology go hand-in-hand—and today I'm going to show you how.

The Numbers in the Minor Arcana

As you know by now, the Tarot deck has 56 Minor Arcana cards—40 numbered cards and 16 Court Cards. The numbered cards separate into four Suits: Cups, Pentacles, Swords, and Wands, with each Suit running from Ace (1) to 10. So, with a little basic numerology, you've got an easy way to get to know the Minor Arcana. Here are a few keywords to get you started:

1. (Aces) New beginnings, opportunity, potential
2. Balance, partnership, duality
3. Creativity, groups, growth
4. Structure, stability, manifestation
5. Change, instability, conflict
6. Communication, cooperation, harmony
7. Reflection, assessment, knowledge
8. Mastery, action, accomplishment
9. Fruition, attainment, fulfillment
10. Completion, end of a cycle, renewal

It also helps to know a little about each of the Suits in the Tarot. You can always revisit those earlier lessons, but here's a quick recap:

- Cups (water) — Emotions, creativity, intuition, relationships
- Pentacles (earth) — Material wealth, money, career, manifestation
- Swords (air) — Communication, truth, intellect, thoughts
- Wands (fire) — Inspiration, energy, enthusiasm

Now, combine what you know about the numbers and what you know about the Suits, and you'll be able to determine what each of the 40 numbered cards means. For example, the Five of Cups is about conflict (5) in love and relationships (Cups). And Four of Pentacles is about stability (4) in finances (Pentacles). *See? I told you it would be easy!*

Now, you might be wondering how to interpret the 16 Court Cards with numerology. Well, it isn't quite as straightforward because the Court Cards don't traditionally have a numerological association. So, it's best to use other techniques for translating this group of Tarot cards (which I cover in my online training program, Master the Tarot Card Meanings. Learn more at **biddytarot.com/master-tarot**).

For now, let's jump into the Major Arcana cards.

The Numbers in the Major Arcana

You can apply the same "Tarot by numbers" technique for the 22 cards of the Major Arcana.

The Fool is the first card, but it starts at 0, and the final card is the World (21).

Each card between the Fool and the World has its own numerological association so you can apply what you know about the numbers to the Major Arcana Tarot cards.

You don't have to know double-digit numerology either. For now, keep it simple and add together the numbers to interpret the single number. For example, the Tower is Card 16 and 1 + 6 = 7. Seven is about assessment and evaluation, an important aspect of the Tower card. Of course, there's a little more to the Tower card than just assessment and evaluation, but knowing the basic numerology will give you a start in the right direction.

While single-digit numerology can be helpful, it can also help to understand the meanings of the numbers up to 21 to add extra depth to your Tarot card interpretations. For example, Death is Card 13, and both Death and the number 13 relate to upheaval; 13 is also a karmic debt number, a sign that we need to learn a life lesson to evolve spiritually.

So, there you have it! You now have an easy way to interpret the Tarot cards using basic numerology as your guide!

Activity

14.1. Explore a Tarot Suit by the Numbers

- Choose a Tarot suit.

- Take out all the numbered cards in that Suit (from Ace to Ten) and lay the cards out in order in front of you.

- Now, take what you already know about that Suit and what you've just learned about the meanings of the numbers. Then, work through each card and map the journey from the Ace through the Ten.

- Note down two to three keywords or phrases for each card using only what you know about the Suit and the numerological association.

- For example:

  - Ace / Cups — New beginnings in love
  - Two / Cups — Partnerships and romance
  - Three / Cups — Socializing with friends
  - Four / Cups — Establishing emotional stability
  - Five / Cups — Emotional losses and disappointment
  - Six / Cups — Harmony in relationships
  - Seven / Cups — Assessment of opportunities
  - Eight / Cups — Moving on from past emotions
  - Nine / Cups — Emotional satisfaction
  - Ten / Cups — Fulfilling relationships

- Once you're done, revisit your keyword chart and add any new keywords to your chart.

If you have time, repeat this activity for the other suits, including the Major Arcana.

Day 15: Interpret the Symbolism in the Tarot

"A symbol is a reminder, something that evokes the echo of an inner experience in the beholder. The deeper and more significant the experience, the more powerful the symbol. It may take the form of an image, a sound, a word, an action, an object, anything that has a concrete existence in the physical world" (Wald Amberstone, co-founder of the Tarot School).

The Tarot is abundant with symbolism. The cards contain symbols from Kabbalah, Christianity, Judaism, Paganism and the Hermetic Order of the Golden Dawn. Understanding what the symbols mean can take your intuitive Tarot reading practice ahead by leaps and bounds, especially if you are a visual person and see the world through pictures and images. The symbolism in the cards can also connect you to your intuition and the subconscious mind, provide a focal point for meditation and opening the third eye. But how do you know what a specific symbol means?

In this lesson, I'll show you the difference between traditional symbolism and intuitive symbolism, plus I'll share interpretations of the most common symbols in the Tarot cards.

Traditional vs. Intuitive Interpretations

When it comes to interpreting the symbolism in the cards and knowing what specific symbols mean in a Tarot reading, you can either tap into the traditional interpretations or your intuitive interpretations.

Traditional interpretations come from the collective wisdom—the commonly held associations for the symbols that have been passed down over many generations, whether it's through religion or other esoteric traditions. Traditional interpretations assign a specific meaning for that symbol that does not differ from person to person.

You can also take the personal wisdom or intuitive approach to symbols, applying the associations you've formed through personal experience. And, depending on how you see life, it might be your personal experiences in this lifetime, or it might be your collective experiences over many lifetimes.

For example, a circle traditionally represents a cycle, infinity, universal or sacred energy, protection, and wholeness. However, you might associate a circle with a commitment, such as marriage, when rings are exchanged. So, when you see a circle in a Tarot reading, you might be intuitively connecting the circle with marriage or commitment.

Remember, neither approach is better than the other. Both traditional and intuitive interpretations of the symbols play a role when you're reading the Tarot cards.

Six Tips for Making the Most Out of Symbolism in Tarot Cards

1. Start with What You Know

Confidence is key when you're learning to read Tarot. So, if you are already familiar with a certain religious or esoteric tradition that will give you clues about what the symbols mean, start there.

For example, if you've already got an interest in Christian symbolism, then think about how it relates to what you see in the Tarot cards.

2. Find Common Symbols and Research Their Meanings

If you look through the Tarot deck, you'll notice a few universal images or symbols shared across the cards. For example, the Tarot has a lot of castles, clouds, and landscapes in its imagery. So, it can be helpful to note these common symbols and then learn the collective wisdom around them. What does a castle mean traditionally? (I've included the meanings of these common symbols later on in this lesson.)

3. Explore Your Personal Connection with the Symbols

Here is where the fun comes in! You can fire up your intuition and connect more with your subconscious when you play with the symbols in the cards.

Let's use the castle as an example. The traditional meaning for the castle is a place that is safe because the walls around it are enormous and insurmountable. But you might look at that castle and those walls and think: "Eek! I love my freedom too much to deal with all those walls." So, a castle might have negative connotations for you.

Explore the symbolism in the cards on a more personal and intuitive level. What meaning do you attribute to the symbol? And how does that differ from the collective wisdom?

4. Compare the Symbols Across Tarot Cards

The beauty of symbolism in the Tarot is that the symbols can take on different meanings depending on the context of the card itself. Let me show you how.

Pull out all the Tarot cards that have castles in them.

Now, look at all those cards and compare how they differ:

- How does the meaning of the castle change as you look at it across different cards?
- Are you standing inside of the castle walls, or are standing on the outside of those castle walls?
- And how does that feel, do you feel included or excluded?
- Do you feel safe or unsafe?
- What's happening around the castle?

For example, a celebration is happening outside the castle in the Four of Wands, but in The Tower, the castle is tumbling down. Are castles as sturdy as you think they might be?

You'll notice that there are many ways in which you could interpret the same symbol!

5. Read Widely

If you're feeling pretty good at this stage, you might be ready to say: "OK, you know what? I know nothing about Kabbalah, but I'd like to learn more and build out my understanding with that extra layer of symbolism." So read books about the Kabbalah and discover what those symbols might mean.

You could also read about mythology, such as *The Power of Myth* by Joseph Campbell. It's a challenging read but also fascinating and abounding with rich symbolism, and I can't help but connect it with the Tarot.

6. Create a Library of Symbols

As you're doing all of this amazing research, keep a notebook of the symbols you're discovering and write what they mean for you. The beauty of building out your own library of symbols is that you're not relying on someone else's interpretation; you're growing your personal experience around those symbols and deepening your relationship with the Tarot.

Common Symbols Used in Tarot

Let's give you a little headstart in interpreting the symbols in the cards. Here are the traditional meanings behind the more common symbols used in the Tarot cards.

Angels

Angels represent a special message that is sure to catch your attention. It's a moment of Divine intervention, so make sure you listen. Also know that something, somewhere, somehow is being done at that moment to help that situation. The angels have taken note and are working on it.

Castles

Castles symbolize protection, stability, accumulation, wealth, and reward. They show that, while there may be a long and difficult journey, the reward or the outcome will be worthwhile. You are slowly but surely working toward a personal goal that will bring a great sense of achievement when you reach it. Castles are often built to protect their inhabitants. Thus, castles can express a defensive mentality, set structures, and specific ways of doing things. They also represent firm foundations and the need to create a solid foundation for your ideas and thoughts before they can manifest into something big.

Chains

Chains mark a connection to something and speak to servitude, bonds, and self-limitation.

Children

Children represent innocence, youth, purity, and naivety. From a very literal perspective, children may represent family or young people.

Circles

Circles represent eternity or cycles that are continually turning and evolving.

Clouds

Clouds often symbolize the element of air and, therefore, are associated with thought, intellect, and abstract thinking. Clouds represent a transitory, short-lived state; they come and go, changing shape as the wind blows. Thus clouds signify that nothing is certain.

Rain clouds bring a sense of doom and gloom, but remember that every cloud has a silver lining. Clouds may also indicate timing, based on seasons. Dark clouds may reflect winter while light clouds or no clouds at all may reflect summer.

Colors

- Black: Endings, the close of a cycle, termination, evil and darkness
- Blue: Tranquillity, truth, thoughtfulness, peace, and calmness
- Brown: Earthy connection, feeling grounded, and stability
- Gold: Vitality, strength, success, wealth, courage, and confidence
- Green: Abundance, prosperity, growth, healing, fertility, and jealousy
- Orange: Courage, pride, ambition, enthusiasm, and energy
- Pink: Compassion, tenderness, harmony, affection, love, and romance
- Purple: Psychic insight, vision, spirituality, higher knowledge, and self-esteem
- Red: Passion for life, lust, willpower, courage, energy, strength, anger, power, and sexual desire

- White: The soul, innocence, purity, naivete, faith, cleansing, peace, protection, and healing
- Yellow: Vitality, positive energy, friendship, enthusiasm, joy, and happiness

Crown

Crowns symbolize attainment, mastery, and public recognition. Crowns also represent the material world and focus on the rational mind.

Cups

Cups are symbolic of water, which denotes emotion, love, creativity, and pleasure. Often, cups reveal opportunities, particularly of an emotional nature.

Dogs

Dogs represent a loyal friend, helper, or close companion.

Fish

Fish represent an idea or thought, often from the realm of the subconscious.

Fruit

Fruit are symbolic of fertility and ideas and plans coming to fruition.

Gardens

Gardens symbolize the beauty of nature, peace, and comfort. They're also safe and relatively private, providing space for retreat, relaxation, and contemplation. Gardens represent the fact that people have the power not only to control nature but also to improve it through nurturing and caring for the earth. Think of an exquisitely landscaped garden that is both aesthetically pleasing and a sustainable food source. Gardens are also living metaphors of perfection. They represent cultivation and growth, all leading to a natural paradise of perfection.

Hands

The right hand represents the conscious mind and masculine energy. The left hand is the subconscious mind and feminine energy.

Infinity Symbol

The infinity symbol looks like a figure 8 on its side. It symbolizes eternal life and shows a harmonious interaction between the conscious and the subconscious.

Keys

Keys provide access to otherwise hidden areas, and therefore can represent secrets and protection. They can also symbolize freedom and liberation.

Leaves

Leaves symbolize growth and vitality.

Light / Lanterns

Light in the form of a lamp or lantern symbolizes spiritual enlightenment, intelligence, deep knowing, and life itself. It represents the search for truth and virtue.

Lightning

Lightning is symbolic of a flash of inspiration. It comes with such power and energy, it creates an often intense experience.

Lion

The lion represents the passionate, primal, and animalistic side of ourselves. It can also be a sign of nobility, pride, and courage.

Moon

The Moon is a feminine astrological symbol of the subconscious mind. It can also reflect the hidden influences and forces present in our lives, just as the moon moves the seas and oceans through the tides.

Mountains

Mountains represent challenges that may stand in the way of your goals. A mountain may also express an ideal you have or wish to attain. Note whether the mountain is high and rocky (a big challenge but also a great reward) or if it is more like a rolling hill (the ongoing challenges we often face).

Paths

Paths are the way to spiritual attainment and esoteric knowledge. They represent a journey or a direction that must be taken to reach a certain goal.

Pomegranate

The pomegranate symbolizes female fertility and sexuality, the inner Goddess, secret knowledge, and rebirth.

Rainbow

The rainbow is a sign of Universal protection, happiness, and ideal states of being.

Scales

Scales represent balanced judgment and objectivity, impartiality and equilibrium. The pros and cons are being weighed up, and decisions are being made.

Serpent / Snake

From Biblical origins, the serpent is a symbol of temptation and secrecy. It also represents wisdom and knowledge.

River / Stream

A river or a stream symbolizes the flow of conscious awareness.

Sun

The sun is a source of light, life force, and energy. It represents radiance, warmth, and vitality.

Thrones

Thrones represent maturity and domination over the chosen realm.

Towers

Towers represent man-made structures and belief systems which are often built upon a false or weak foundation.

Water

Water symbolizes the subconscious and emotions.

Wreath

A wreath represents victory and accomplishments.

Personalizing Symbols

Symbols carry accepted or shared meanings. So, if we see a lion, we know it means passion and primal energy. But, as we've discussed, symbols also carry personal meaning.

As a child, I had a soft toy that was a lion. He was like my protector and would make me feel better when I was sick or give me courage when I felt scared. So, a lion, to me, represents protection and courage. But what if you had been on an animal safari in Africa and had a near-death experience with a ferocious lion!? You might see the lion as a symbol of fear and overwhelming power.

One of my readers, Rob, shared this very personal story about the Tower card:

> **When I first started doing Tarot readings for myself, I was afraid to have the Tower card come up in a spread. I used to let out a gasp! For me, it's the card for 9-11 when two jet planes were hijacked and smashed into our World Trade Center (Twin Towers) buildings. I live an hour from Ground Zero. This terrorist attack changed my life, my neighbors, and my country. A sense of our freedom was lost. Sudden change, disaster, upheaval. Later on, as I became more educated in Tarot, I began to see the Tower as a part of life, and it's not so frightening anymore. And that's positive!**

So, in addition to learning about the shared meanings of symbols in Tarot, it is also important to explore your personal meanings. They're just as relevant as the established, traditional meanings.

Using Symbols in a Tarot Reading

We can use symbols in a Tarot reading in a number of ways.

You can use the shared meaning of a symbol to delve deeper into the Tarot card. For example, the lion in the Strength card tells us that this is about primal energy and passion—but you can use your own personalized meaning, too. So, if I were to notice a lion in the cards, I might be drawn back to my childhood, to feelings of protection. This is useful during a reading when a particular symbol catches your eye. Take it as a sign that your inner voice is talking to you and has used the symbol to channel a personal message to you.

You can also use personalized symbolism with a client during a Tarot reading. Ask your client, "What does this symbol mean to you? What have been your personal experiences to date, or what does this symbol mean to you now? Does it bring joy, fear, sadness, anger? What emotions does it generate?"

Don't be shy to ask your client questions during a reading. Doing so can be powerful as it facilitates a client's deeper understanding of themselves and the reading's key messages.

Activities

15.1 Get Up Close & Personal with the Symbols

- Choose a common symbol from the Tarot cards, like a castle, an angel, or a cloud. Write or draw the symbol in your Tarot journal.

- Now, for the next ten minutes, write everything that comes to mind about that symbol. It might be keywords, memories, songs, other symbols, stories, fairy tales, dreams, and/or personal experiences. Let your mind run free and without judgment.

- Then, based on your brainstorm, choose two to three keywords based on your personal associations with the symbol selected. You may like to work through each symbol, building your very own symbol keyword chart.

15.2 Compare the Symbols Across the Cards

- Choose a new symbol, or use the same symbol as above.

- Now, go through your deck and find all the Tarot cards that feature this symbol.

- Ask yourself:

  - What are the similarities across the cards?

  - What are the differences?

  - How does the symbol appear in each card? (Is the symbol far away in the distance, or is it in the foreground?) And how does this influence the card's meaning?

  - Are there other symbols shared across the selected cards?

  - Write your insights in your Tarot journal.

Day 16: Interpret the Stories in the Cards

Did you know that each Tarot card holds a unique and individual story? At first glance, it might appear like a static picture. But as you explore each card in more detail, you will notice various stories and tales emerging that reveal deeper insights about that card's meaning.

Stories have always been a primal form of communication. They are timeless links to ancient traditions, legends, archetypes, myths, and symbols. They connect us to a larger self and universal truth. Learning to interpret the story in a Tarot card is one technique that I have found to be useful and surprisingly simple to do. In fact, even now, I find that if I draw a blank during a reading, I will start to tell the story of the card, and as I do, additional insight emerges.

Revealing the Story in the Cards

In any good story, the scene is set and then something happens—a conflict, a setback, a challenge, or surprising good fortune. Add in a bit of action and, eventually, there is an outcome or resolution and a moral to the story. Well, we can use these same narrative principles to reveal the stories behind each of the Tarot cards!

So, let me show you how you can break down the scene, action, outcome, and moral for each Tarot card's story. We'll start by setting the scene.

Scene

Describe exactly what you see in the picture.

- Who is in the picture?
- What is in the picture?
- Where is the picture situated?

Action

Ask yourself open-ended questions about what is happening in the picture. For example, "What is the man reaching out to?" or "Where are the children going?" Look closely at the picture.

- What is happening?
- Who is doing what?
- Is there conflict or harmony? What has created it?
- What might have happened before the snapshot? And after?

Outcome

Here is where you may need to be a little more creative in your responses.

- What results from the actions taken?
- Is it a positive outcome or a negative outcome?
- What might happen next?

Moral

- What is the moral of the story?
- What is the deeper meaning?
- Ultimately, what does this card mean for you in this reading?

What you will find is that often your story is a mixture of fact and fiction. You will be describing what you see but also interpreting it based on your intuition and creative mind. The stories you tell may differ from the stories other people tell about the same card, but that's the beauty of the Tarot! It's all about trusting your intuition and going with your gut feeling about what YOU see in the cards.

Let's Bring a Story to Life

To show you how to reveal the story in the cards, let's work with the Three of Wands.

Scene

Here, we see a man standing with his back to us, atop a grassy hill. He wears red and green robes and a bandana around his head and is holding three sprouting sticks or wands. The man gazes out over a large body of water at three sailing ships traveling along. A mountain range sits in the far background.

Action

This man is an entrepreneur. He watches the ships pass along the trading route from a high above on his hill. He is already successful in business but is continually on the lookout for expansion and growth (the sprouting wands). He knows challenges lie ahead (the mountainous terrain in the background), but he looks to these challenges with excitement and anticipation.

Outcome

Because of his desire to grow his business, this man has achieved international success and business is booming. Nothing is impossible for him right now!

Moral

By expanding your horizons, you can create growth and wealth in your own life.

There you have it! A detailed narrative with an exciting (and memorable) message, all crafted from a single card. I encourage to you to select a card or two and try it yourself. It's also a great way to get the creative juices flowing and develop specific Tarot card meanings and keywords. For example, we now know the Three of Wands is about growth and expansion, business, and enterprise. Then, once you have developed your story for a particular card, you can then derive its deeper meaning.

Creating Meaning from Stories

You can also use the story during a Tarot reading. Telling the story may help to convey to your client (or to you) the card's deeper meaning. Sometimes, the story may be actually playing out in his or her life, giving an insight into what may happen next. Sometimes it can provide a useful analogy that helps them understand or apply the card's message. Here are a few ways you use story in your readings.

Use the story to ask questions. Let's look back at our Three of Wands example. What questions might you derive from the story we created? My curiosity gets pulled to the ships in the distance, so I might ask my client what ships he/she has sailing? What projects are on the go? What challenges are up ahead? What is growing and expanding? Where do new opportunities lie?

Use the story in the card to give a kick-start to your intuition. I find this helpful if I am initially uncertain about how to interpret a card in a Tarot reading. Let's say the Three of Wands showed up in response to "Where is my relationship with Joe heading?" I might be a little stumped as to why this card is appearing here, so I tell the story to see where it will go:

"OK, we can see this man standing here, two feet on the ground, not going anywhere just yet. But he is looking out across the sea to another land, another territory. There is a lot of promise and hope there. He's thinking about where his best opportunities lie, not just for now but in the future."

Ah! Here we go. Intuition is kicking in...

"Are you thinking about a longer-term future with Joe? Are you considering taking the next step with him and embedding your commitment with him even more? And look, see those hills in the background? You know there are going to be some challenges ahead, but you are willing to deal with them as they arise."

Ah, phew! You see? All we need to do is relay the story, and our intuition does the rest.

Activity

16.1. Create Your Own Stories in the Tarot Cards

- Select three Tarot cards.
- For the first card, use the Scene—Action—Outcome—Moral formula to build a story from the card.
- Now that you've got the hang of it, write a fairy tale using the second card. Start with, "Once upon a time..."
- With the last card, write a story about yourself, using your present-day circumstances. It might be about your work, a relationship, an event, or a bit of make-believe!

Day 17: Meditation with the Tarot

Meditation offers a way to go even deeper into the meaning and symbolism of each Tarot card as it allows us to bypass our often-noisy conscious mind and dive into the subconscious mind and connect with our higher self. By relaxing our mind and letting go of our constant thought processes, we open up the pathway to our subconscious mind and begin to tap into a higher level of knowledge and insight. We allow our intuition to guide us and, in doing so, building a much deeper understanding of the Tarot cards.

A Tarot meditation typically begins with a general relaxation of the body and the mind, before moving deeper into the image of the selected Tarot card and exploring its messages.

Tarot Card Meditation in Seven Steps

Step 1: Select a Tarot Card

If you are using the Tarot card meditation simply to explore the Tarot card meanings in more detail, then select a card you want to connect with more deeply (or choose one at random).

You can also select a Tarot card based on what's important to you right now. For example, if you're single and want to bring love into your life, you may select the Two of Cups or the Lovers. Or, if you're on a path of spiritual development, you may select the Hermit.

Step 2: Set up the Environment

Choose a time and a place where you won't be disturbed for at least twenty minutes. Make sure you're comfortable, the phone is on do-not-disturb, and all other distractions are out of the room. Then turn your attention to the mood of your space. You might like to play meditation music or simply have silence. You could diffuse some essential oils and dim the lights.

When you're ready, sit in an upright position. (Lying down will most likely just put you to sleep!) And keep your Tarot card in front of you.

Step 3: Focus on the Breath

Once you are comfortable, bring your attention to your breath.

Breathe in through your nose and, as you do so, notice the sensation of your breath in your nostrils. Take a deep breath in and then breathe out through your nose, again focusing on the sensation in your nostrils. Continue breathing and focusing your attention on the sensation of the breath.

At this stage, if you notice any thoughts coming into your mind, just observe them and then imagine them floating away like clouds. If your attention wanders, gently draw it back to your breath.

Step 4: Relax

Now, shift your attention to your body. As you breathe in, feel the oxygen entering your body and filling you with pure energy. And as you breathe out, imagine relaxation simply flowing through your body.

Scan your head, neck, shoulders, arms, torso, hips, legs, and feet, and feel the relaxation flowing through all the way down to your toes. Now, you are relaxed and at peace.

Step 5: Move into your Tarot Card

Bring your attention to the Tarot card in front of you. Gaze softly at the card and take in five deep breaths. Again, if you notice any thoughts coming into your mind, just observe them and then imagine them floating away like clouds. Bring your attention back to your breath and the Tarot card in front of you.

Imagine the card growing larger and larger until the figures and the imagery are almost life-size. See yourself stepping into the card. Look around you. What do you see? Who is in the card with you? What objects are present? What colors stand out to you? Take a moment to touch an object in the card and feel its texture. What do you hear? Take a deep breath in and smell the air. Is there something edible in the card? Taste it.

Now, imagine yourself as one of the figures in the card. Become that person or archetype. How does it feel, being this person? What does this character think and sense? How do they move and behave? What is their attitude toward the scene around them?

Begin to speak as if you are that character. What do you have to say? What is your message? What advice do you have to offer?

Take another look around you. What makes you feel good? What gives you energy? What, if anything, makes you feel anxious, concerned, or upset? Notice any sensations in your body at this point and release any tension that may have formed.

Look for the different objects and symbols in the card now. How can they be used? What are they here for? What is their symbolic meaning?

Glance around you one last time. What do you see now that you didn't see before?

Your work is almost complete. Step out of the figure and then step out of the Tarot card. Watch as the card becomes smaller and smaller, returning to its normal size.

Step 6: Awaken

Acknowledge the work you have done here and know that you can return to this place of peace and insight at any time. Begin to bring your attention back into the room, taking in two deep breaths and feeling the energy returning to your feet, your hands, and your body.

Open your eyes (if they were closed), feeling refreshed and energized.

Step 7: Take Note of Your Insights

Immediately after your Tarot card meditation, take note of what you saw, heard, thought, or felt during the meditation. Record it all in your Tarot journal.

Guided Meditations with the Major Arcana Cards

If you want to deepen your connection with the Major Arcana cards and bring their potent energy more fully into your life, then you'll love my audio program, Soul Meditations.

Soul Meditations is a series of guided meditations designed to lead you on a tour of your own intuitive mind as you discover a profound, yet practical, way for you to connect with the 22 Major Arcana cards of the Tarot.

I invite you to experience a guided meditation with the Fool, taken directly from Soul Meditations, for free. Go to **biddytarot.com/meditate-free**.

And to learn more about Soul Meditations, go to **biddytarot.com/meditate-soul**.

Additional Ways to Meditate with Your Tarot Cards

If you're working with a Major Arcana card like the Chariot, include the following questions in your meditation as you step into the character:

- What drives you? What motivates you?
- What are you so fiercely determined to achieve right now?

Mantras are also an effective way to create a focal point and to concentrate your insights. Select one keyword for the card you are studying and repeat it over and over in your meditation. For example, a keyword for the Fool may be "Beginnings," so repeat, "Beginnings, beginnings, beginnings," to deepen your insight into what this means for you and for the card.

You may even like to set up the scene in the card in real life and meditate on its energy. For example, for the Ace of Cups, place your cupped hand under running water and experience how it feels spilling over the sides of your palm and around your fingertips. Clear your mind and be wholly present with the physical experience.

Tarot Meditation in Practice

Here's a personal story from Louise, who comments regularly on my Tarot blog (**biddytarot.com/blog**):

I have done a lot of these Tarot meditations over the years and have found the insights from them often profound. Sometimes they take me in a slightly different direction to before, or they show me a new aspect I had yet to consider. I still remember a lot of them, years and years later, whereas often a book interpretation is forgotten as soon as the book is placed back on the shelf!

I'd like to share one of these meditations with the Four of Swords. It wasn't that the figure in the card spoke to me, or anything moved or changed or came to life, but when I went into the meditation, my eye was drawn to the black line that runs down the center of the stained glass window in the card. Then I was shown the black line under the Knight's tomb, and really, that was it! Sounds really simple and uneventful, and would be easy to dismiss as useless and pointless, but it proved beneficial to my understanding because I hadn't paid attention to these black lines before!

I came out from this meditation and thought "Humph! That wasn't very impressive," but instead of dismissing this detail as trivial or unworthy, I began to really start to work with it. This meditation was many, many years ago now, and to this day I still remember the "lesson of the black line"! My inner teacher showed me that no detail on the Tarot should be overlooked, no detail is arbitrary! The black-line is important to a deeper understanding of the card, for it separates the saint from his kneeling subject in the window picture, and with very close observation it can be distinguished that the letters PAX appear above the head of the saint, the old Roman word for peace. The saint has peace; the kneeling follower is separated from it by a thick black line! Similarly, the Knight is separated from his fourth sword by a thick black line under his 'tomb,' and it shows us that the Knight and the follower in the window do not have inner peace, but they are trying to find it.

> **Meditation offers a way to go even deeper into the meaning and symbolism of each Tarot card as it allows us to bypass the conscious mind and dive into the subconscious mind and connect with the higher self. We allow our intuition to guide us and in doing so, we build a much deeper understanding of the meaning of the Tarot cards.**

I guess all it really did was confirm the book reading of the card, but it has given me a personal understanding which got into my brain at a much deeper level. I haven't forgotten it, and the thick black line always jumps out at me on this card. It confirmed the meaning in a personal way and showed me that our inner world CAN teach us. After all, the word "intuition" when broken down is inner-tuition, the inner teacher.

What will your Tarot meditation tell you that you don't know already?

Activity

17.1 Meditate on a Tarot Card

- Select a Tarot card and work through each of the seven steps outlined above, making sure to note your insights following the Tarot card meditation.

- If you find value using Tarot meditations, you may like to use it on a regular basis to move deeper into a card or better understand what it's telling you.

- Try my free guided meditation with The Fool at **biddytarot.com/ meditate-free**

Day 18: A Card A Day

You now have the opportunity to call upon your personal experiences and intuition to deepen your understanding of the Tarot cards. The "Card a Day" exercise is one of my personal favorites and, I believe, was most helpful in bringing the cards to life in my own Tarot studies.

A Card A Day in Four Steps

Step 1. Select a Tarot Card

First, decide how you would like to select a Tarot card for each day.

Random pick: Ask what you need to know for the day ahead and select a random card from your deck. You'll get the benefit of learning the Tarot cards as well as specific insight for the day ahead.

Ordered pick: If you're keen to work methodically through the Tarot deck, you may wish to look at each card in order. For example, you might begin with the first card of the Major Arcana and move through until you reach the end. This approach has the benefit of being able to cover each and every Tarot card (provided you stick with it for 78 days, of course!).

It also doesn't have to be a new card every day—it could be every three days, each week, etc.

Step 2: Study the Tarot Card

Once you have selected a Tarot card for the day, study it in detail for five minutes.

What is your first impression of the card? How do you feel when you look at it? What thoughts or feelings immediately come to mind?

What images stand out to you? Are there people in the card and what are they doing, thinking or feeling? What symbols are present? What colors do you notice? Look at the details of the picture. What did you miss at first glance? How does this change your view of the card?

What do you know about the card? What keywords have you already selected? What do you know about the corresponding astrological sign, the Major or

Minor Arcana, the Suit, and the numerological and elemental associations?

Take note of your initial thoughts and observations. Write down:

- The first five words or phrases that come to mind as you look at the card.
- A sentence that describes what is happening in the picture.
- The main emotion expressed in the card.

And finally, if this image were on the front of a greeting card, what would the message inside say? Write your ideas in your Tarot journal.

Step 3: Go About Your Day, Being Conscious of Your Tarot Card

Go about your day as you usually would, and as you do, stay conscious of the situations, events, or people that may align with or have something to teach you about your "card of the day."

For example, if you selected the Page of Swords, you may be on the lookout for people who are curious and energetic in what they do. Or you may identify a particular situation with the Page of Swords' energy—the start of a new project or an opportunity to speak publicly.

You may even choose to *be* the card you have selected. If you were to express the Page of Swords' energy today, you may choose to ask lots of questions. Write down how this made you feel afterward and whether you noticed anything you would not normally associate with the activity.

Make sure you carry around your Tarot journal to note down your experiences and observations throughout the day.

Step 4: Write Down Your New Insights About the Tarot Card

By the end of the day, you will have a number of specific and personal experiences, situations, and even people you have seen throughout the day that encapsulate the key messages of your selected card.

Return to your notes about your Tarot card and add your new insights. Be specific. What happened? Who was involved? What did you personally experience? How did the card and the situation make you feel?

Combine the insights you have received into one or two sentences. For example, the Page of Swords represents someone who is curious, energetic, and eager to move forward with a new project. Personalize that description with what you have learned throughout your day.

Build the "card a day" practice into your usual daily routine, and you'll find your Tarot learning accelerates exponentially!

The Card a Day Activity in Practice

One of my readers, Cheryl Janzen, tried this activity out for herself. Though she had already studied the Tarot for six years, she found a lot of value in the "card a day" activity. She shares her insights below:

> **The activity is wonderful and provides an in-depth personal meaning to each Tarot card. At first glance, I would have never thought of the interpretation as such. Doing this exercise each day not only assists with learning tarot card meanings, but it enables one to lead a richer, more fulfilling life. It opens your mind, perhaps giving you 'inside' information. I felt like I had just finished an insightful counseling session. With more clarity of mind and affirmation of my path, I actually slept better than I had for weeks. It was as if my higher mind proclaimed, "Way to go—you chose the untrodden path that is your divine right, and you are a much happier person for it."**

Cheryl chose to select a Tarot card at random, asking, "What do I need to know for the day ahead?" She drew the Nine of Cups. Here is what she noted in her own words as she followed the steps outlined above.

The first five words or phrases: Be grateful, keep emotions in perspective, be realistic, and appreciate all you have right now.

One sentence that describes what is happening in the picture: The figure sits proudly on a bench in a protective stance, after considerable hard work and emotional turmoil; he has sufficient faith in himself to take a risk and step off the beaten path to attain his dream.

The main emotion expressed in the card: Fulfillment.

If this image was on the front of a greeting card, what would the message inside say: The message would come from Napoleon Hill: "Every adversity, every failure, every heartache carries with it the seed of an equal or greater benefit."

My first impression of this card is self-satisfaction. The thoughts and feelings that immediately come to mind are a happy ending (shown by the character's smile and proud stance, and the sunny-yellow background).

The image that stands out to me is the crossed arms of the character. I wonder if he has closed off his heart to some extent, perhaps through being overly protective and possessive of his achievements.

The symbol that grabs my attention is the red hat—the color representing his passion, and the style representing the prosperity that has been attained.

At first glance, the detail that I missed was the bench, representing his solid establishment. This detail does not change my view of the card, rather it confirms my impression.

She later noted her insights about the card at the end of the day:

While in quiet contemplation at a family dinner this evening, I realized that I mirrored the figure in the Nine of Cups with my crossed arms protecting my heart and closing off any discussion regarding my family's devotion to traditional religion versus my spirituality and metaphysical studies. I am content and at ease sitting on this bench. I am proud that I stepped off the path to walk my own journey. The Nine of Cups affirms my path and feelings of satisfaction.

In closing, Cheryl noted how the Card a Day activity helped her to develop an even stronger understanding of this Tarot card:

The textbook meaning of the tarot cards is a fantastic guide for interpretation. For instance, the colors of the card provided clues, such as the blue representing the extent of emotions surrounding the issue, the red representing my passion for my chosen path, and the yellow representing the self-fulfilling outcome.

However, ultimately, intuition and open-mindedness provided an accurate reading. This activity teaches me the value of keeping a non-judgmental attitude and an open mind when reading the tarot cards.

How will the "card a day" activity help you!?

Activity

18.1. Draw a Card a Day

- Draw a Tarot card for the day and interact with it using the above suggestions. Take note of what you have learned in your Tarot journal.

- Again, if you find value using this process, I recommend that you incorporate this activity into your ongoing Tarot learning (after the 31 days are over).

Day 19: Good Cards, Bad Cards

The imagery in the Tarot cards is so strong and powerful that we often sense its energy before we really understand what's going on behind the scenes. Show the Ten of Swords or the Death card to any Tarot reading client, and you will see their expression change from intrigue to shock or anxiety. Or, on the flip side, draw the Sun or the Two of Cups card, and your client can't wait to hear what's coming up.

The imagery in the Ten of Swords, Tower, Devil, Hanged Man, Death, Three of Swords, and the Seven of Swords lead us to think that they are inherently "bad" or negative cards. While the imagery in the Sun, Star, Two of Cups, Ten of Cups, Ten of Pentacles, and Lovers depict highly positive scenes, which leads us to perceive them as "good" Tarot cards.

But, are Tarot cards really either "good" or "bad"?

The first thing to acknowledge is that it is not the imagery itself that makes it a good or bad card. It is how we perceive that imagery. While our first reaction might be, "Oh no, that's a 'bad' card," we need to push ourselves beyond that first reaction and delve deeper into exploring all sides of the card.

What's more, every card in the Tarot deck has light and shade—in other words, it has both positive and negative aspects. Take the Devil, for instance. Yes, this card highlights issues of attachment and entrapment, but it can also show a very strong bond between two people or an exciting sex life.

As we've discussed, the Tarot is very much like life itself. Dark times have their silver linings, and even good things have their drawbacks. For example, I land a dream job, but it means I have to relocate and leave my friends. Or I miss out on an opportunity, but it ends up being a blessing in disguise.

Another way to look at it is how we harness the energy of the cards in our life. If we bring too much or too little of a card's energy into our life, it can easily turn a "good" card into a "bad" one. Take the Sun. It is a very happy card, but what might happen if its energy becomes excessive? Too much of the Sun's energy may lead to egocentric behavior or being overly optimistic about a situation.

When "Bad" Cards Show Up in Positive Positions (and Vice Versa)

We've touched on this briefly in our discussion of the Court cards, but a card's position in the Tarot spread you're using should be integral to your interpretation. But where we often trip up as Tarot readers is when a seemingly "bad" card turns up in a positive position or a "good" card turns up in a negative one. Some common positive and negative Tarot spread positions include:

- Strengths / Weaknesses
- Advantages / Disadvantages
- Opportunities / Obstacles

In a Celtic Cross spread, oftentimes it is the Problem, Advice, Hopes/Fears, and Outcome positions that can cause problems. If we only see Tarot cards as 'good' or 'bad,' then these positions are always going to confuse us. But it doesn't have to be that way.

Reading "Good" Cards and "Bad" Cards in Four Steps

1. Let Go of the Idea of Good and Bad Tarot Cards

Really, there are no "good" and "bad" Tarot cards in the Tarot. Every Tarot card has its light and shade, its positive and negative aspects. When you start to let go of the need to attribute black-and-white interpretations to the cards, you allow more possibilities to shine. So, make a commitment to yourself now: there are no good and bad Tarot cards!

2. Let Go of Your Assumptions

Let's say the Two of Cups turns up as a "problem" in a relationship reading. *Hmmm... But this relationship is brand-new. How could a new relationship be a problem!?* Perhaps that relationship is inappropriate or unhealthy for some reason—perhaps it is an affair or with a colleague or a best friend.

You move to the next card—the Five of Swords. Now, if you believed in "bad" Tarot cards, you might take it to mean that this new relationship is doomed!

Fortunately, you know there are no bad Tarot cards, so you decide to look closer. Ah, now you see. The Five of Swords may be a sign that arguments are a healthy part of this relationship and actually help the couple to understand each other.

You can't assume that a particular card is always going to hold positive or negative energy for an individual's life. The Devil might just be a very desirable card if someone enjoys a bit of bondage and role-playing, or the Hierophant may be a complete turn-off to the commitment-phobic.

3. Explore the Light and Shade of a Card

If you draw a seemingly negative card in a positive position, think about, "How could I make this card work for me, not against me?" For example, the Seven of Swords is often about trickery, deception, and betrayal. Not a particularly helpful energy in this form, huh!? But what if we turned this around and thought of the card as strategic and symbolic of "working the system" while also employing the principle, "Do no harm." Now we're talking!

It's the same for positive cards in negative positions. Consider: "What might too much of this positive energy look like? How could this be to my detriment?"

4. Look on the Bright Side of Life

Let's say you draw the Five of Pentacles as an opportunity. First reaction? How could poverty be an opportunity? Well, it was for author and spiritual teacher Eckhart Tolle! He lived below the poverty line for several years and, though it was difficult, this period of his life allowed him to become so much closer to his spiritual self.

Always consider how something seemingly negative could actually be a blessing in disguise. And on the flip side, always consider whether there is a downside to something that is seemingly positive. Life is just like the Wheel of Fortune, constantly turning from positive to negative to positive again.

Activity

19.1 Expand Your Associations with the "Good" and "Bad" Tarot Cards

- Pick out three to five cards that you feel represent the most "negative" cards of your Tarot deck. For each card, come up with at least one meaning that is more "positive" or that allows you to connect with its energy in a positive way.

- Now, select three to five cards that you feel are the most "positive" cards in your deck. This time, come up with at least one interpretation of each card that may be a shortcoming or a negative aspect of the card.

- Write these interpretations down in your Tarot journal and keep them nearby for future readings. If you ever have a "good" card come up in a negative position, or vice versa, you'll now have a handy reference to make it easy to interpret.

Day 20: Reversed Cards

If you're a Tarot beginner, you might be wondering why on earth you would want to read with reversed Tarot cards and double the amount of information you need to learn to become a good Tarot reader. I get it—I totally do.

But here's the thing: *You don't have to learn another 78 Tarot card meanings to master reversed Tarot cards.* You only need to learn the methods that will help you take the upright energy of the card and apply it to the reversed energy of the card. (It's easy to do, and I'll show you how in this lesson.) And once you master those few methods for interpreting reversed Tarot cards, here's what's possible for you...

- You can double your insight and expand your understanding of what the Tarot cards mean for you in a reading.

- You can see the light and shade of a situation and identify where to release any blocks.

- You can delve into what's happening within you versus what's happening around you—perfect for knowing where to make the most impactful changes.

- And you can even get a simple "Yes" or "No" in your Tarot readings.

Do you have to read with reversed cards to be a good Tarot reader? Nope. However, reading with reversed Tarot cards will open up a whole new layer to your readings and provide you the opportunity to go even deeper with your intuitive insights.

Let me show you how.

4 ways to interpret reversed cards

1. Internalized Energy
2. Too Much or Too Little Energy
3. Blocked Energy
4. Upside-Down Imagery

I've chosen these methods because...

- They offer a balanced perspective—not all "doom and gloom" but not all sugary-sweet either.
- They serve to empower the client.
- They are simple to learn and apply in your readings.
- They work!

These are the exact same methods I use in my personal and professional Tarot readings, and that I teach to my students in my Tarot training courses.

Method #1: Internalized Energy

At the heart of it, Tarot cards are energy. Each and every card is an expression of energy in its many forms.

For example, the Empress is an expression of abundance, fertility, and mother energy. When we encounter the Empress in our everyday lives, we might experience her energy as nurturing and taking care of others or successfully bringing a new project to life.

An upright Tarot card represents "externally expressed energy." That is, the energy of that Tarot card is expressed outwardly in the world and experienced in your external environment and in your relationships with people and situations.

Reversed Tarot cards are internally expressed energy. That is, the energy held within ourselves, or more private or even secretive energy. For example, the upright Empress may represent taking care of others, whereas the reversed Empress may represent taking care of yourself. To simplify this method even further, take the upright meaning of the Tarot card, and then add "self" or "private" to your interpretation.

What I love most about this technique is that there is no "good" or "bad" message here (unlike the traditional reversed card meanings which focus on the opposite of the upright card meaning). It's simply showing you where the energy is being felt.

This technique can also show where changes need to be made or where action needs to be taken. If your Tarot reading is mostly upright cards, then you know you're dealing with external situations and your relationships with others. If your Tarot reading is mostly reversed cards, then you know you're dealing with yourself, and any required actions or changes need to happen within you first.

Method #2: Too Much or Too Little Energy

Reversed Tarot cards can often point to an imbalance in energy, identifying the areas in your life (or your client's) that are holding too much or too little of the cards' corresponding energy.

Take the Queen of Wands, for example. Upright, she represents a confident person who enjoys social situations. However, what does it look like when there is too much or too little of this confident, social energy?

Perhaps she is over-confident and domineering, especially in social settings (too much of the Queen of Wands energy), or perhaps she is a wallflower or "shrinking violet" when in a room with others (too little of the Queen of Wands energy).

When I'm reading the cards in this way for a client, I'll often pose it as a question: "What role does confidence in social settings play for you? Do you feel overconfident, or do you want to find a quiet corner where you can hide?" And, I'll often follow up with, "How can you make confidence in social settings work for you?" That is, how can you bring this energy back into balance and alignment? Super empowering, right!?

Method #3: Blocked Energy

This method is similar to the "too much or too little energy" approach, but with a slight difference. Energy can often appear in our lives, but it can get blocked or isn't being expressed in the most constructive way possible.

For example, the reversed Temperance card may indicate that you are seeking out moderation and harmony in your life, but right now, there's something blocking you from fully experiencing that energy positively.

Ask, "What's getting in the way of you achieving moderation and harmony?" That is, identify what is blocking the energy. Then, ask, "How can you release any blockages associated with moderation and harmony?" Perhaps you need to reconnect with the mantra, *Everything in moderation.* Perhaps you need to pick your battles to create more harmony. Maybe you need to let go of the expectation that there will always be perfect harmony in all things.

Finding the answers to these questions may be as simple as holding an open dialogue, or you may pose these questions to the Tarot to see what comes up.

Method #4: Upside-Down Imagery

I love working with the pictures in the Tarot cards, especially when I want to connect more intuitively with the situation.

If a Tarot card appears in the reversed position, look at the imagery of that upside-down card, and see what comes to you intuitively. For example, in the Ten of Swords reversed, it appears as if the swords are falling out of the man's back. Perhaps the pain that has been inflicted in the past is now finally being released, and the client can move forward into a new cycle—especially since this is a Ten, the end of a cycle.

Or in the reversed Page of Pentacles, the coin looks as if it might slip out of the man's hands. His grip is not very tight, and he doesn't seem to be concentrating. Perhaps it is a sign that, without the necessary discipline and focus, money is just slipping out of your hands.

This technique is particularly powerful if you're a visual person. The images often create an instant link between your conscious and unconscious mind, helping you to connect with your intuition.

So, there you have it—four of my favorite methods for interpreting reversed Tarot cards.

If you want to master the reversed Tarot cards and learn not just four, but *eight* methods, then you'll love my Master the Tarot Card Meanings online training program (https://www.biddytarot.com/master-tarot/).

In this signature program, I'll show you how to interpret upright and reversed Tarot cards from the heart, not just the book. And I'll teach you the must-know systems that make learning Tarot super easy. By the end of the program, you'll have what it takes to become a confident and intuitive Tarot reader who everyone raves about!

How Do You Know Which Method to Use?

Now, with so many ways to interpret a reversed Tarot card, you're probably scratching your head and wondering, "How on earth am I going to know which method to use and when!?"

Well, that's why it takes years and years of practice to become a good Tarot reader! Nonetheless, here are a few tips to help you know which method to use:

Mentally Agree to Use One Method Only

Tell the Universe prior to a reading how you are choosing to read reversals. For example, "I am going to interpret all reversals in this reading as blockages." This way, the Universe will present your message to you in alignment with your intention.

Go with Your Gut Instinct

Sometimes you just "know" what the card refers to. Your intuition may be guiding you toward a specific interpretation, or you may be drawn to a combination of interpretations as listed above.

Look at the Other Cards in the Reading

Look for themes across the different cards in the spread you are using. For example, the Four of Cups reversed combined with the Hermit may suggest that your client is spending too much time alone and shut off from the world around them. On the other hand, the Four of Cups reversed combined with the Nine of Cups reversed may indicate that your client has lost their connection with their inner selves and exterior opportunities are also unfulfilling.

Draw on Your Personal Experience

Sometimes, it really does just come down to experience. For example, I know now that whenever I see the Three of Cups reversed in a relationship reading, nine times out of ten, it indicates that there is a third person involved and it is usually the client who is that third person.

To help you build your own experience, seek feedback from your clients to understand how the cards are playing out in their lives. Do this not only during or directly after the reading but also a few weeks or months later. Find out how a particular card came to life for you or your client and understand what it looked and felt like.

Activities

20.1 Get some reversed cards into your Tarot deck

- My favorite method is to cut the deck into three piles. Turn one pile from top to toe, 180 degrees, so that those upright cards will become reversed cards, and vice versa. Then put all the piles back together and shuffle. Or you might prefer to do a "messy pile" shuffle by spreading the cards out on a table haphazardly and moving them all around before picking them back up into a neat pile. Or something else! Again, there is no 'right' way of shuffling. Choose what feels best to you.

20.2 Play with different ways to interpret reversed cards.

- Choose one card that you feel comfortable with and reverse it. In your Tarot journal, note everything you can about the imagery of that card in the reversed position. Then, write out four interpretations of the card, based on the four methods you learned above.

  - Decide which method of reading reversals feels best to you.

20.3 Take your Tarot readings to a deeper, more profound level

- Check out my online Tarot training program, Master the Tarot Card Meanings at **biddytarot.com/master-tarot**

Day 21: Create Tarot Card Combinations

If you want to go from 'good' to 'great' as a Tarot reader, then make sure you learn how to interpret multiple Tarot cards into one combined meaning. As your Tarot reading skills and talents improve, you'll be able to look at a reading, find interesting card pairings, and then create meaningful interpretations that draw upon the combined meanings of those Tarot cards. This is truly where the magic happens!

To get you started, I'm going to show you how to practice creating Tarot card combinations, and later, when you start doing your own readings, you can put these into action.

How to Create Your Own Tarot Card Combinations

Working with Tarot card combinations requires you to first select a pair or group of Tarot cards and then to develop the meaning and interpretation for the combination of those cards.

Select Your Tarot Card Combinations

There are two primary ways to select your Tarot card combinations: a "conscious" selection of the cards or a random draw.

A conscious selection means that you draw one Tarot card from your deck and then consciously choose another Tarot card that aligns with your selected card. Consider the general meaning of the card you are studying and ask yourself:

- Which Tarot card reinforces the card's meaning or makes it stronger?
- Which card opposes the card's meaning or makes it weaker?
- Which other cards give this card a completely different meaning?

For example, I randomly select the Four of Wands. This card often denotes celebrations in the home or family or a stable relationship. Now, a card that may reinforce the Four of Wands is the Ten of Cups—a card of a happy home life filled with love and harmony. The Ten of Cups simply makes the Four of

Wands even stronger in its positive message.

A card that may oppose the Four of Wands is the Three of Swords—a card of grief, sorrow and loss. A family celebration may end in a loss (like news of a pregnancy, soon followed by news of a miscarriage). Here we see that initial positivity of the Four of Wands being weakened by the Three of Swords.

And finally, a card that may give the Four of Wands an entirely different meaning is the Eight of Wands—a card of travel. This combination may indicate an overseas celebration, such as a wedding in a tropical location. It still embodies the general significance of the Four of Wands, but this combination now offers a different angle on its traditional meaning.

Don't worry if the combinations don't come to you straight away. Go through each card, one at a time, until you start to find more meaningful combinations. Once you get into the groove of selecting cards and matching them with other card combinations, it becomes a lot easier and is a fun activity to do.

If you start to find this task *too* easy, then consider doing a random draw.

A random draw means that you randomly select two cards from your deck and then develop the meaning associated with that pair of cards. This can be a lot more difficult because the cards may initially not make a lot of sense together. However, the exercise does encourage you to look deeper into different card pairings and to get a little creative in your interpretations.

For example, let's say I drew the Sun (a positive, energetic card) and the Four of Swords (a passive, restful card). On first glance, it may seem that the passive nature of the Four of Swords opposes the active nature of the Sun. However, upon further reflection, I would interpret this as a sign that rest is needed now in order to re-establish the energy of the Sun card. Perhaps this is a good time for a vacation or doing something you really enjoy. Once you have made your initial selection of the pair of Tarot cards, dig deeper into the combined meaning for those cards.

Delve Deeper into the Combined Meaning

Start by interpreting each card separately and then combining those meanings (just as we did in the examples above). What does the first card mean? How about the second card? How do these two meanings combine?

Day 21: Create Tarot Card Combinations

Do they reinforce each other or oppose each other?

Next, consider the following interactions between the cards:

- Suits: How does a Cups card (emotions) interact with a Pentacles card (practical matters)?

- Minor / Major Arcana: How does a Minor Arcana card (day-to-day events) interact with a Major Arcana card (life lessons)? Or a Major with a Major? Or a Minor with a Minor?

- Numbers: How does a Two (a partnership) interact with a Nine (nearing completion)?

- Symbols: What symbols are common across the selected cards, and what does this signify?

- People: How do the people in the cards interact with one another? For example, is it a male and a female? Or is it a Page and a King? Do they face one another or turn away? What does this signify?

Let's take a look back at the examples from the first step, when we selected the cards.

The Four of Wands and Ten of Cups is interesting from a numerological perspective. The Fours symbolize stability and certainty, while the Tens symbolize completion. The pairing of these cards may indicate a solid relationship progressing to the next or ultimate level of commitment, like marriage or family.

Look also at the people in each of these cards. Both feature a couple. In the Four, the couple faces us, whereas, in the Ten, the couple stands with their back to us. Could this represent a journey, perhaps, of coming forward with a relationship and finally reaching a place of peace where the couple can finally sit back and enjoy the moment of completion?

The Four of Wands and the Three of Swords is an interesting elemental pairing as well. Wands (fire) and Swords (air) are both considered active and support each other. This turns the original interpretation on its head and suggests that perhaps the flow of events goes the other way. From loss and sorrow comes happiness and stability; thus, the loss actually supports eventual happiness.

The Four and Eight of Wands pairing is also interesting from the Suits perspective. This time it is a combination of Wands and Wands, strengthening the concept of energy and forward movement. This would likely add to the party atmosphere of an overseas wedding!

And finally, the Sun and the Four of Swords. If we look at the people in these cards, we notice a stark contrast between the young boy in the Sun to the older man in the Four of Swords. Perhaps this is then about leaving behind the "adult" and embracing the inner child in yourself by taking a break from work and engaging in more fun activities.

If you would like to take it a step further, you can do so by exploring card combination meanings for different contexts. For example, what would the Four of Wands and the Ten of Cups mean in a relationship reading? In a work reading? A spiritual reading? How about a family reading? Or a financial reading? This exercise will really start to test your creative abilities!

Overall, Tarot card combinations will facilitate more effective Tarot reading skills, enabling you to draw upon the various layers and interactions within a Tarot reading. Not only will you be able to interpret what each card means, but you will also be able to draw relationships between each card and create a much more comprehensive and insightful reading for your client.

Tarot Card Combinations in Practice

From time to time, I'll post two Tarot cards on Facebook (**facebook.com/ biddytarot**)and Instagram (**instagram.com/biddytarot**) and invite readers to comment on possible interpretations. In one such instance, the cards were the Moon and the Seven of Swords. It was wonderful to see so many responses to the same two cards—a further reminder that it really comes down to what YOU see in the cards, rather than what a book tells you to see in the cards.

Here are some of my favorite responses:

> **"There is something happening without your acknowledgment or consent. The Moon card suggests that the action or incident is happening under your nose while the Seven of Sword card is trying to tell you that someone is doing something behind your back."**

"Since the Moon is the card of illusions, I would interpret this as the querent is subconsciously concerned, worried, or fearful that someone in their life is cheating or stealing from them even though that is not what is actually going on."

"Paranoia or unseen treachery."

"In a love reading, I would say it is a very emotional and spiritual betrayal that the querent never dreamed a loved one would be capable of doing. Financially, it represents theft and profit from a trusted colleague or friend. The person receiving the reading may have sensed something was wrong but believed it couldn't be possible. This could also represent serious criminal activity from a loved one, such as murder, robbery, and assault, with the querent as the victim."

"To me, these cards combined suggest self-betrayal or self-sabotage. The Moon card governs our intuitions, fears, and unconscious thoughts, the dim and murky dreamlike margins of our own minds, our own selves. There's an element of the shadow self in this card. Combined with the Seven of Swords, with its implications of betrayal, deception, and escape, I would interpret these cards to mean that on some deep, hidden level the querent is working against his or her own best interests."

Activity

21.1 Create Your Own Tarot Card Combinations

- Using the method above, create your own Tarot card combinations.

  - To help get you started, I have selected five Tarot cards for you to work with (see below). Find another Tarot card that reinforces the selected card, and another card that opposes the selected card. I have filled in the first one for you.

Card	Reinforcing Pair	Opposing Pair
Four of Swords	Four of Cups—in quiet meditation	Nine of Swords—tormented by inner thoughts
Two of Pentacles		
Star		
Queen of Wands		
Ace of Cups		

Keep your Tarot card combinations for future reference in your Tarot journal. You can refer to it when you see those combinations come up again in your readings. The reading itself may also highlight further Tarot card combinations that you have not yet discovered.

Section 2 - Congratulations!

✔ You now know the meanings of the Tarot cards!

✔ You can name each Tarot card.

✔ You have two to three keywords for every Tarot card.

✔ You can build your own interpretations by looking at the symbols, numbers, and stories within each card.

✔ You have personalized your understanding of the Tarot cards.

✔ You understand each Tarot card individually and as part of a bigger system through patterns and connections.

✔ The cards are beginning to feel like a part of YOU.

Section 3: How to Read Tarot for Yourself and Others (Days 22 to 31)

Apply everything you've learned so far. Conduct your first Tarot reading, see the story in the cards, and connect with your intuition. Step into your confidence as a Tarot reader!

Ready to Read? Of Course You Are!

In this next section, we're going to immerse ourselves in actually *reading* the Tarot: we'll talk through everything from setting up your reading space, how to shuffle and lay out your cards, to how to choose the right spread. Then we'll deep dive into the interaction between the cards, how to ask the right questions to get empowering answers, and most importantly, how to build your trust in your intuition.

We'll begin by creating a sacred space for you (and your intuition) to engage with the Tarot.

Day 22: Create the Sacred Space

Imagine these two scenarios for a moment:

Scenario 1: You're having your Tarot cards read in an open booth at a busy festival where people keep interrupting your reader to make a booking. It's noisy, and you can barely hear the reader over the booming music from the Zumba demonstration on a stage nearby. *(And yes, this kind of scenario really does exist! I'm not making it up!)*

Scenario 2: You're having your Tarot cards read in a quiet room with the door closed. Soft music is playing in the background, and you sip a cup of herbal tea while your attentive reader tunes into your energy throughout the reading.

Which experience would you prefer? I know which one I would choose (and which one would make me never return).

You see, the space in which you conduct your Tarot readings is incredibly important to both you and your client. It's what creates trust between you and allows the energy to flow freely throughout the reading, setting the stage for in-depth insights and transformation. Get the space wrong, and you'll risk losing trust, losing credibility, and worse, losing clients.

And guess what? It's just as important to set up a sacred space when you read for yourself. Grabbing your deck while in the middle of making the kids breakfast, giving it a quick shuffle, and throwing down three cards while you flip pancakes is the equivalent of reading at a booth next to a Zumba stage. We've all done it, and it most often leads to confusion and re-drawing cards because we can't make sense of (or don't like) what we're seeing.

Sacred space and ritual bring a beautiful depth and energy to your readings. It *feels* good. Creating such a space is also a great way to read consistently, as you start to really look forward to this special time!

So how do you create a sacred space for your Tarot readings? You need to consider four key elements:

- Physical space
- Mental space
- Emotional space
- Spiritual space

Let's dive into each of these, and I'll share with you how you can create a sacred space within each one.

A Sacred Physical Space

The physical space represents the tangible environment: the room, seating arrangements, where you lay out the cards, and so on.

Choose a reading space where both you and your client feel safe – where you can have a confidential conversation and you can both be fully present with one another. If you are in an enclosed space, close the door and put up a "do not disturb" sign so that you will not be interrupted halfway through a reading. If you are in a public space, like a café, park, library, airport, just make sure you still have some level of privacy. And if anyone else starts to get a little curious and listens in to your reading, you might gently invite them to go elsewhere so you can have some privacy.

I love to do my personal readings out in nature, a sacred space in itself. Often, I'll just pull together a few crystals that are calling to me that day, go into the garden to pick some flowers or find interesting things on the ground, and arrange them on my Tarot reading table. I allow myself to be guided by what feels good on the day, creating my sacred space without an elaborate fanfare.

You may like to decorate your sacred Tarot space with candles, crystals, pictures, and beautiful fabrics. However, don't feel obliged to do this if it's not your personal style. Personally, I like to keep it simple—I have my Tarot cards, crystals, and laptop, and that's about it! And remember: tidy space, tidy mind. Clear away any clutter and only have what is absolutely necessary and honors the sacred space.

A Sacred Mental Space

A sacred mental space is one where you (and your client) are bringing a clear and focused mind to your Tarot reading. It's about letting go of any extraneous issues that may be occupying your thoughts, like shopping lists, an angry conversation, or picking up the kids at 3pm.

I always like to start a Tarot reading with a few deep breaths to center myself and bring my focus to the reading at hand. I also ask my client to be very clear about their question and situation *before* we start the reading. When reading for yourself, treat yourself as the client and ensure you are clear on your question when addressing the cards.

If you are reading face-to-face, you may like to have your client take a few deep breaths with you. And if they seem particularly anxious or distracted, ask them to write down what's on their mind for a couple of minutes then place it in a box nearby. Reaffirm that those thoughts are "parked" for now.

Finally, I love to play meditation music to bring about focus, especially with binaural beats. It will help to calm the mind, draw you into the present, and increase your focus on the reading.

A Sacred Emotional Space

A sacred emotional space is one where you and your client are coming to the reading without any strong, negative emotion. Instead you both feel clear, focused and relaxed.

For example, if you've just had a huge argument with your partner and are still fuming about what he said to you, it's important to clear away this negative emotion first before pulling the Tarot cards. Otherwise, you may not be a clear channel for intuitive connection if you are still caught up in the emotion of that previous experience.

A sacred emotional space is also one where you and your client feel safe and 'held' in the presence of one another. This means that, as a reader, you have an open heart and are ready to listen deeply to the needs of your client. You can feel empathy and compassion, without being swayed by your own emotions or thoughts.

To create a sacred emotional space, take some time to center yourself through the breath. You might simply guide your client to, "Breathe in love, and breathe out fear."

And to create a sense of emotional safety and trust, build a rapport with your client before you begin a reading. I often start with a casual conversation or asking whether they've had a Tarot reading before. It helps to break the ice and let the client know you're a regular, everyday person who's here to help.

A Sacred Spiritual Space

A sacred spiritual space brings a special energy to your Tarot readings and will help you to connect with the Universe and your intuition during a reading.

A simple way to do this is to set an intention before the reading, to connect with your Higher Self and your inner wisdom. Or you can call on your guides or angels to hold the space for you and your client and to support you in becoming a Divine channel for the reading. Some Tarot readers also use a prayer or affirmation to prepare, such as, "I open myself to becoming an instrument of truth and insight to honor the divine spirit within all of us."

You may also like to clear your chakras before a Tarot reading to connect deeply with your spiritual self. Chakras represent our energy centers in the body and opening each of these prior to a Tarot reading can assist in creating a very deep and insightful reading.

To help connect you with your intuition and create a sacred spiritual space, I recommend listening to my 15-minute Confidence Booster Meditation (download it for free at **biddytarot.com/meditate**). It's designed specifically for Tarot readers who want to clear their mind, ground their energy, and connect with Spirit before a Tarot reading.

Activity

22.1 Set Up Your Sacred Physical Space

- Collect items such as crystals, candles, and herbs that resonate with you and enhance your Tarot readings. Have some fun with it! Take yourself on a creative date to the woods, the beach, or your local metaphysical shop.

- Clear the clutter from your reading space and give it a good energetic cleanse.

- Once you've set up your space, do a reading for yourself and journal on how you felt and how you connected with the cards in your new sacred environment.

Day 23: Ask Powerful Questions

Asking the right questions in your Tarot readings is the key to gaining insight and unlocking the answers you seek. After all, when we ask good questions, we get good answers. (And similarly, when we ask vague or misguided questions, we get vague or misguided answers.)

Consider these two scenarios:

Scenario #1: You ask the Tarot, "Will I ever find love?" and you draw the Hermit. *Oh, no*, you think, *I won't find love and will live a life of solitude.* You end the reading feeling completely bummed because you really wanted to find "the one" soon and now it looks like it'll never happen.

Scenario #2: You ask the Tarot, "What can I do to create the love life I truly desire?" Again, you draw the Hermit. Well, now, that changes things a bit, doesn't it? If you want to find "the one," you should first spend some time on your own, reflecting on the type of relationship you really want. By being on your own, you will come to a deep realization about your inner resources and how they can support you in finding true and authentic love. This time, you end the reading feeling empowered and optimistic, knowing exactly what it is you need to do to find the kind of love you truly want.

Of those two Tarot readings, which would you prefer? I know which one I would choose.

You see, the quality of the questions in your Tarot readings is directly linked to getting the answers that can help you to shape a path forward and manifest your goals and dreams.

Now, while I wholeheartedly believe that guidance from the Tarot can support you in any situation, as we saw above, there are just some questions NOT to ask the Tarot.

Ten Questions NOT to Ask the Tarot

1. Will my lover leave his wife? (Or any other question about another person's life that is not directly related to you.) Questions like these stir up issues around privacy and accuracy: privacy because you are delving into someone else's private life without their permission, and accuracy because you will still be seeing the situation from your/the client's perspective and not necessarily the situation as it is.

2. Will I win the lottery? The lottery is a game of chance and there is very little that you can do to influence you winning, except for buying a lottery ticket. So, leave that outcome up to chance and the little colored balls bouncing around in the big glass bubble, rather than consulting the Tarot cards.

3. Does my ex hate me? (Or any other question that deals with such negative emotion.) "Hate" is such a strong word, and it often implies that you are blaming someone else for taking out their negativity on you. And, let's say you did get the answer, *yes, your ex hates you,* then what?? What can you do about it? It becomes so disempowering. Instead, focus on constructive questions such as, "What can I do to improve on my relationship with so-and-so?" or "What do I need to improve within myself to create better relationships with others?"

4. When will I die? (The same goes for "How long will I live?") Apart from being incredibly morbid, this is not an appropriate question for the Tarot because the Tarot is intended as a guide and there is really no "guiding" with this type of question. Knowing the answer will not help.

5. What is the name of my soul mate? The Tarot cannot accurately name significant people in your life (at least not that I'm aware of!). Sure, it can identify what type of person is best suited to you, but it will not hone in on just one person in a universe of 7 billion people. I also believe that many people have the potential to be your soul mate, so why just focus on one?

6. Am I pregnant? Leave any sort of diagnosis, prognosis, or treatment advice to the medical professionals. The Tarot cards are not a proxy for a visit to the doctor. Yes, they can highlight if there is a possible issue or concern, but go and see your doctor to get checked out.

7. Will my wife's cancer go into remission? (Or any other question specifically about health and the health of others, even loved ones.) Not only is it unethical to predict health outcomes, it's generally an outcome that you cannot influence. So rather than consulting the Tarot cards about what will happen, refocus the question on what you can do to support your loved one through this difficult time and maximize their chances of recovery. Similarly, if you require health advice, consult a doctor.

8. Should I take the job? (Or any other "Should I..." type of question.) You need to take responsibility and accountability for your own life and your own decisions. Don't hand over your agency and free will to a stack of cards! It is better to ask the Tarot, "What is the impact/pros and cons if I take this path?" or "What can I expect if I do XYZ?" That way, *you* are still making the decision, not the Tarot cards, and you're focused on how you can manifest the outcome you want.

9. When will I get married? Ok, this probably isn't a terrible question to ask the Tarot, particularly if you feel comfortable with answering timing questions or have a tried and tested method for doing so. However, the trouble with this type of question is that it assumes you will get married at some point in your life. But what if you don't?

I recommend rephrasing the question to something like, "What do I need to know about getting married?" or, "What is the potential of my relationship with so-and-so?"

10. Will I win the court case? When an outcome is completely out of your hands, you are better off asking the Tarot what you can do to improve your chances of success or what you need to know about the situation at this time. What's more, Tarot readers are typically not legal professionals and are therefore not in a position to provide legal advice. Stay on the safe side and invest your money in legal advice rather than a Tarot reading on the topic.

OK, Then What Makes A "Good" Question for The Tarot Cards?

As we saw in the last section, the types of questions you ask can shape your reading for better or worse—it can even impact the entire experience and how you feel about it! Asking the *right* types of questions can make for a fantastic, informative, and empowering Tarot reading. So, what constitutes a good question?

The best questions will elicit information that empowers you to make the best decisions for yourself or situation. They focus on what you can influence or change in a positive and constructive way. They keep you (or your client) in the driver's seat!

Good questions are often open-ended, providing space to explore different options and possibilities. But they are also detailed and specific, allowing focus and direction. Good questions focus on yourself rather than others. They create a feeling of responsibility and accountability, reinforcing that you have free will and can indeed shape your own destiny. Let's take a look at how you can shape your questions to deliver a compelling reading.

How To (Re)Phrase A Tarot Question

In most cases, an initially inappropriate question can be slightly tweaked or rephrased to make it more informative or inspiring.

- What do I need to know about...
- What do I need to do to achieve...How can I improve my ability to...
- What do I need to change in order to...
- What is the potential for...
- What is standing in the way and how can I best overcome it?
- What role do I play in so-and-so's life/issue?

So, if the initial question is something like, "Will I get married this year?", you may like to rephrase it to, "What do I need to know about getting married this year?" or "What do I need to do to improve my chances of getting married this year?" It's a small tweak, but it can fundamentally change your understanding of the reading.

You can also include a timeframe in your request to increase the specificity of the question and the answer. For example, "What do I need to know about my finances in the next six months?" or "Will I meet a romantic partner in the next three months?" However, it is generally best not to set a timeframe beyond a year as a lot will have changed after this time.

That said, the question does not have to be perfectly worded. Consider what you really want to know or understand about a situation, and then formulate your question(s) accordingly. What's most important is that you are clear about what you're asking the Tarot cards and that you are empowered to positively impact your future.

So how do we ask good questions?

Ask Open-Ended Questions

Questions that can be answered with a simple "yes" or "no" are closed questions. They're fine if you want a fast answer, but the trouble is that they don't allow for any deep reflection or exploration of a situation; they simply state what is or isn't going to happen.

By asking the Tarot open-ended questions, you'll get far more interesting insights. For example, instead of asking, "Will I find a new job?" you might ask, "What has been keeping me from finding a new job, and how can I release these blockages?" The first question can only be answered "yes" or "no." The second question invites deeper reflection and opens the space for understanding how you can manifest your goal of finding a new job.

To ask open-ended questions, avoid starting the question with "will," "when," and, "should," and instead ask, "what," "how," and, "why."

Get to The Heart of The Question

Let's say your client starts the session with the question, "What's my soul mate like?" Now, sure, you could launch right into that reading by drawing a few cards and seeing what comes up. And sure, you might end up with a description of a potential soul mate. But will the reading really be insightful and helpful for the client?

Now, let's say you ask a few more questions to understand what's really on your client's mind and how you can help. Perhaps you find out that your client is single right now and has been having trouble finding the right partner for her. You realize she wants to know what her soul mate is like so she can recognize him when he appears.

Well, now you have more information to work with, and now you can craft a reading that will be much more helpful. Instead of asking the Tarot, "What's my soul mate like?" you now ask, "What signs might I see when I have met the right partner?" or "What can I do to attract the right partner for me?"

Instead of taking a question on face value, explore it! Unpack it, and get to the heart of what your client, or you, are really asking. You'll find that you can then address those deeper questions and deliver more meaningful insight.

Ask Follow-Up Questions

Every question can be broken down into follow-up questions that serve to explore the different elements of the original query. For example, a question like, "How can I live in alignment with my soul's purpose?" can be broken down into these follow-up questions:

- What is coming into my conscious awareness about my soul's purpose?
- How can I discover my soul's purpose?
- What is my soul's purpose?
- How am I presently living in alignment with my soul's purpose?
- What inner work do I need to do to align with my soul's purpose?
- What resources are available to me that will help me to live in alignment with my soul's purpose?
- What will bring me closer to my soul's purpose?
- What might stand in the way of me fulfilling my soul's purpose and how can I overcome it?

And so on.

Now, do you notice what's happening here? As we start to break the original question down into follow-up questions, we also start to form the beginnings of your very own customized Tarot spread. You could literally draw one card for each of the questions above, and you'd have an in-depth and fully customized Tarot reading!

So, for your next Tarot reading, check in with yourself, first: *Am I asking the right question of the Tarot? Is it open-ended, and does it allow for deep exploration and insight? Does it get to the heart of the matter? And are there follow-up questions I could ask?*

Ten Powerful Questions to Ask the Tarot

To help you get started with asking empowering questions, I've put together a list of questions to ask the Tarot that will take your readings to the next level. Use these questions on their own, in your daily reading, or as part of your customized Tarot spreads.

1. What is coming into my conscious awareness about... [insert situation]?

2. What might I experience if... [insert possible scenario]?

3. What does my soul need from me right now?

4. How can I live in alignment with my highest good?

5. What new opportunities are emerging?

6. What soul lesson am I discovering right now?

7. Where are my blind spots?

8. How can I create more [insert desired feeling] in my life right now?

9. What actions do I need to take to manifest my goals?

10. What matters most in my life right now?

Activity:

23.1 Practice Rephrasing Disempowering Questions

- Think of a closed question you're tempted to ask the Tarot (or even a question you've already asked that generated confusing results). Something that starts with *when, will*, or *should*. Now, write out three different ways to ask that question in an empowering way—and remember to open your new questions with *what, why*, or *how*.

- Do a three-card reading using one of your new, powerful questions.

- Write your insights into your Tarot journal.

Day 24: Choosing a Tarot Spread

When you go into a Tarot reading with a specific question in mind, it pays to be mindful about which spread you choose. But there are so many Tarot spreads to choose from! How do you choose the right one for the query?

First, you need to get to the heart of the question. What's really being asked? For example, if you ask, "Will I get back with my ex?" are you asking "Is this the right relationship for me?" or "Is it time to move on for my highest good?" Once you start to unpack that question a little more, you will have a better understanding of which Tarot spread will answer your *real* question and give the most insight. I like to read using custom spreads rather than premade ones because I find it helps to unpack a big question in a really helpful way—and you can use the same technique!

Create your own Tarot spread by breaking down that big question into small follow-up questions and, *voila*, you have your very own Tarot spread that will get to the heart of that question. The thing to remember is to *keep it simple!* You don't have to have an elaborate twenty-card spread. Clarity and alignment are key, which means the follow-up questions you come up with will make a great foundation for your custom spread.

If creating spreads isn't your thing, that's OK too! You can start with a simple three-card spread, like one of my faves: "Past-Present-Future."

1. Past-Present-Future Spread

The Past-Present-Future spread is one of the most popular Tarot spreads out there—probably because it is also one of the most simple and insightful. It works well for both general and specific situations where you want to understand the timeline of events related to that situation. Let's break it down:

- The Past shows you what has led you to where you are now.
- The Present shows you where you are now.
- The Future shows you where you are heading, based on where you are now.

Can you see a pattern here? While it may be a Past-Present-Future spread, it's actually all in the context of the here and now. And do you know why? The here and now is where you can make the changes you need to create the future you want! Let's take a spin through an example reading to see the Past-Present-Future spread in action.

Reading a Past-Present-Future Spread

Your client asks: "What do I need to know about my career?" So, you pull three cards, one marking the past, another for the present, and a third that will speak to the future.

Past: Eight of Wands. You have had a very fast progression through your career. You may have been required to travel by air frequently as a part of your job.

Present: Four of Cups. You are at a point now where that fast-paced work life no longer suits you, and you're starting to turn down these opportunities.

Future: Ten of Cups. You see a future where you can spend more time with your family at home. Travel is no longer an option, and work may become less of a priority to you; your family is your ultimate focus.

Now, combine your insights. *You're going through a transition in your career, where regular travel and a fast-paced work life no longer meet your needs. You are establishing new boundaries in your career so you can prioritize your family instead.*

2. Situation-Problem-Advice Spread

The Situation-Problem-Advice Spread is another of my favorites because it's all about creating the outcomes you most desire.

You can use this spread for both general and specific situations to gain insight into what you need to do to get a situation back on track.

Let's break it down:

- The Situation shows what you are experiencing right now.
- The Problem speaks to the core issue or challenge you face.
- The Advice suggests what actions you can take to achieve your goals.

Here's an example of the Situation-Problem-Advice spread at work.

Reading a Situation-Problem-Advice Spread

You are your own client this time around, and you want to know: "How can I trust my intuition more?" You pull three cards and lay them out in front of you.

Situation: Eight of Pentacles. You are working hard to become more intuitive, taking lessons, and doing repetitive activities to improve.

Problem: Knight of Swords. The core issue is that you are striving to be more intuitive through repeated action and pushing forward.

Advice: Hanged Man. At the heart of it, you need to surrender to your intuition and look at this goal from a new perspective. Intuition is not about *doing* but about *being.*

Combine your insights. *Instead of trying so hard to be more intuitive, surrender to the process and allow your intuition to be a part of your life.*

3. The "No Spread" Spread

The "No Spread" spread is fun, flexible, dynamic, and perfect for all kinds of readings.

It's called the "No Spread" spread because it has no predetermined positions. Instead, the previous card determines the placement. Simply draw the first card, interpret it, and then create the next position from that card. Let me show you how.

Reading a "No Spread" Spread

Your client wants to know: "What do I need to know about my new romantic relationship?"

Shuffle the cards and spread them out into a fan shape, so you can easily select cards from the fan as you go.

First Card: Page of Cups. You are in a phase of discovery and curiosity, and you are exploring new emotions and feelings in a way that you haven't experienced before.

After you interpret the first card, what new question comes up? In this case, the Page of Cups might lead you to ask, "What am I learning as part of this relationship?"

Second Card (What am I learning as part of this relationship?): Queen of Wands. You're learning to become more expressive, compassionate, social, and energized. Your heart is opening, and you are welcoming this person into your life.

Now, what new question comes up? In this case, the Queen of Wands might lead you to ask, "How can I take this expressive and compassionate energy and create a positive relationship?"

Third Card (How can I take this expressive and compassionate energy and create a positive relationship?): Two of Cups. You can create a deeper connection with each other by seeing the good in one another. If you are embodying the Queen of Wands energy, how can you see the Queen of Wands in your partner also?

Continue to ask further questions based on the cards drawn until you feel the reading is "complete" and you have the insight you need.

Personally, I'm a sucker for Tarot spreads! I love structure, and I love knowing exactly what each card relates to. However, not everyone is like that, and you might be someone who prefers less structure, opting for the No Spread Spread instead. Try each method out and see what works for you. Or, you can simply choose to draw a few cards to see what comes through! The key is to make sure you're choosing a spread or layout that's in alignment with your question, and that will provide you the clarity you need.

I have included more suggestions for easy three-card spreads in the back of this book.

Activity

24.1 Try the "No Spread" Spread

- Ask an empowering question and lay down the first card. Interpret the card and allow it to lead you to the next question.

- You don't have to interpret the whole reading at this stage (you'll do that in the next section). Just move from card to card and let each one guide you to ask a new question.

- Write your questions and cards pulled (as well as your card interpretations) in your Tarot journal, and make some notes on how it felt to do such a dynamic spread. You may also like to take a photo of the final spread or draw a diagram of how you laid out the cards for future reference.

Day 25: Do a Tarot Reading

Your space is set, and you're ready to read. First things first: shuffle your deck!

Shuffle and Lay Out the Cards

There are many ways to shuffle the cards. You can use just one method or a mixture of methods. Here are just a few:

Overhand shuffle. This is the most common way of shuffling a deck of cards. Holding the deck in one hand, use your other hand to shuffle the cards from one side to the other of the main deck.

Cutting the deck. Cut the deck into several piles and then bring those piles back together again.

Messy pile shuffle. Lay the cards face-down on the table and then use your hands to spread them out in a big, messy pile. Then, bring the cards back together into one pile.

If you are working with reversed Tarot cards (which I don't recommend until you have mastered the upright cards), there are a number of ways you can introduce reversed cards to your Tarot deck. First, cut the deck in two and turn one pile 180 degrees (that is, upside down with the cards still facing downward) and then shuffle. Alternatively, you can place your cards in a messy heap and shuffle them around until some are upside down. Gather them up again to form a neat pile. Personally, I have the client shuffle the deck with the overhand shuffle, cut the deck into three piles, turn one pile 180 degrees (as I work with reversals), put them back into one pile and then shuffle them one last time.

When it comes to laying out the cards, you first need to decide whether you will lay the cards facing you or the client.

Will the Cards Face You? If you deal the cards to face you, it makes it easier to read the cards. Often, an image will catch your eye and tell a particular story which you can then convey to your client. I also believe that as the reader, it is important that you see the cards as they are being laid out, rather than your client, since it is you who is interpreting the cards.

Will the Cards Face Your Client? If you deal the cards to face your client, they can see the images and symbols themselves and may become more engaged in the reading. This strategy can be useful if you want to include your client in interpreting the cards. For example, before you explain what the card means, you may have them study the imagery and tell you what they notice or feel when they see the card. Often, the imagery has messages not only for the reader to convey to the client but also for the client to pick up on their own. Even if the client does not know of the Tarot, getting them to study and interpret the pictures can be an invaluable way of accessing their subconscious messages. There are a number of ways in which you can select the cards for the Tarot reading, after having shuffled the deck.

Work from the top of the deck. Select the first card from the deck and continue to select the next card in this manner.

Fan the deck and select the cards. Push the cards out to resemble a large fan, and then request the client selects cards at random, using their left hand (thus tapping into the subconscious mind).

Cut the deck and select the cards. If using a three-card spread, cut the deck into three and turn over the top card from each pile.

Personally, I use the first method when I read online, but when I read face-to-face, I use the second method as it engages the client more in the reading. Choose what works best for you. Then it's time for the fun part: interpreting the reading!

Interpret the Reading

First, study the full layout. What feelings do you get when you see all the cards set out in front of you? Do the cards convey an overall "mood"? Where do you think the reading is going? Are there mostly Major Arcana cards, Minors, particular Suits, numbers, or symbols? Look for the patterns and themes that may give you some clues as to the general message of the reading.

Then, go through each card, from left to right, and interpret what it means for you.

Start by looking at the card and pay attention to its energy and any intuitive hits you might receive right off the bat. Examine the picture and describe what you see.

What's happening?

- How does it relate to you (or your client) right now?
- How does the card relate to its position in the spread?
- How does it connect to your client's question?

As you go through each card, keep listening to your intuition and allow your inner voice to guide you to the most meaningful interpretations and messages within the cards.

If you draw a blank with one or more of the cards in the reading, leave it and move on. You may find that the card will make more sense after you have explored the messages of the other cards in the reading. Or, it may simply be "filler" in the reading, and the other cards that stand out to you will play a more significant role in telling the story. Alternatively, if you are unsure about the meaning of a particular card, ask, "What is this card trying to tell me?" and pull another card to answer it.

Draw on the Tarot card meanings you have developed through the exercises in this book. While you will have your favorite Tarot books as a backup, use your personal notes first to create a more intuitive reading.

If you need a little extra support, consult the Ultimate Guide to Tarot Card Meanings (**biddytarot.com/ultimate-tarot**) to discover the traditional meaning of the card. Remember, though, only refer to the book after you have fully explored the card intuitively. Promise?!

Explore the Interactions Between the Cards

Once you have interpreted each card, look at all the cards in the Tarot reading, as if they were pages of a storybook.

- How does the energy flow from one card to the next?
- How do they engage with each other?
- Does the central figure look toward one side or the other? If so, what (or who) is being given attention, and what is being ignored?

Or does the central figure face forward? Perhaps there is a choice that must be made between two options, as represented by the cards on either side.

Day 25: Do a Tarot Reading

Let's take a closer look at the following three-card spread. Before we move through it together, I want you to examine these three cards. What can you infer based on the interaction between the cards?

The Chariot faces head-on, yet two opposing forces, represented by the two sphinxes, pull him. On the one hand, he can remain stuck where he is (see how the figure in the Eight of Swords remains still?), or he can move forward, leaving behind that which is troubling him (note how the figure in the Eight of Cups moves in the opposite directions to the other cards).

In a relationship reading where one card gets drawn for each person involved, see how the figures in those cards relate with one another. Are they looking at each other? Are they looking away? Are they gesturing to one another? What are their reactions to each other? This will often tell you a lot about the dynamics present within the relationship.

Let's look at another example— this time for a relationship between a mother and daughter. Just like before, I want you to take a look at the cards on your own to see what your intuition has to say about the dynamic between mother and daughter. Then we'll walk through it together.

The mother appears as the nurturing and caring Empress, while the daughter appears as the Fool, ready to explore the world. But look at what stands in between them: conflict and tension! Both have pure intentions—the mother to care for her daughter, and the daughter to find herself on a new path—but they are at loggerheads because they are failing to see eye-to-eye and they are not even trying to understand each other's point of view. The daughter desperately wants to retain a connection, given that the Fool remains looking towards the Empress in this layout.

Studying the interactions between the cards can be helpful, so keep this technique up your sleeve throughout the reading, as it will prove to be very useful.

Bring It All Together

Once you've explored the patterns across the spread and the meanings of each individual card, it's time to summarize the reading's key messages. This is your moment to provide an integrated view or overall summary of what's happening in the client's life and what they need to know to move forward. Take your client on a high-level journey of where they've come from, where they are now, and where they're heading. Identify the problem, the solution, and the outcome or the answer.

Finally, circle back to the original question and provide an answer based on the cards.

So often we get to the end of a reading and think, "Phew, all done!" Yet we have missed an important detail of what the client wanted to know in the first place! And check in with your client, too: "Does this provide you with the answers you need? Is there anything else we need to explore here? Can I clarify anything?"

This process might seem very involved on first read, but trust me, it will get much easier and much more natural the more you practice it.

Activity:

25.1 Practice a Tarot Reading

- Apply what you've learned so far! Ask a powerful question and pull three cards. Look for the flow and interaction between the cards, and see what your intuition reveals to you.

Day 26: Discover the Celtic Cross

The Celtic Cross Tarot Spread is one of the most popular and commonly used spreads out there. It's in nearly every Tarot book, and it's the spread most Tarot readers want to know about. But did you know it's also one of the hardest Tarot spreads to interpret correctly?

The Celtic Cross is a complex spread—I'm sure it feels like a big leap from the three-card spreads we have been working with so far—and many Tarot readers miss the deeper insights it has to offer because they don't give enough attention to all the different interactions happening within the Celtic Cross. If you want to be the Tarot reader everyone raves about, you'll need to master the dynamics between the cards and tell the story in your Tarot reading.

It's OK if you feel a bit intimidated right now. I'm with you every step of the way, and in this chapter, I'm going to show you not just the layout and positions of the Celtic Cross, but I will also show you exactly how to read the Celtic Cross by diving into its most critical relationships.

The Celtic Cross Layout

OK, let's get to the basics. Here's your standard Celtic Cross layout (see card layout on the next page):

Card 1—The Present: This card represents what is happening to your client (or you) at the present time. It also reflects the querent's state of mind and how they may perceive the situation.

Card 2—The Challenge: This card represents the immediate challenge or problem facing the querent. This is the one thing that, if resolved, would make life a lot easier. Even if you draw a "positive" card in this position, consider it carefully as it will still represent a challenge.

Card 3—The Past: This card represents the events that have led up to the present situation and may provide some indication of how the challenge came about.

Card 4—The Future: This card represents what is likely to occur within the next few weeks or even months. This is not the final outcome, simply the next step on the journey.

The Celtic Cross

Card 5—Above: This card reflects the querent's goal, aspiration, or best outcome with regard to their situation. It is what your client is working toward consciously as they attempt to resolve the issue.

Card 6—Below: This card reflects your client's subconscious and delves deeper into the core of their situation. It symbolizes the underlying feelings and trends and can show what is truly driving the querent. This card may bring a surprise message to your client, particularly if they are not deeply connected to their inner being. (Watch out for reversed cards here, which are likely to indicate that this message is "unknown" to the querent.)

Card 7—Advice: The advice card takes into account all that is happening within the querent's life and presents a recommendation for what they can do to address their current challenges.

Card 8—External Influences: This card highlights the people, energies, or events that will affect the outcome of the question and are beyond the querent's control.

Card 9—Hopes and/or Fears: This is perhaps one of the most difficult positions to interpret. Keep in mind that hopes and fears closely intertwine, therefore that which we hope for may also be that which we fear—so they may fail to happen. Sometimes it's useful to draw a second card for clarification after the reading has been laid and to read the two together.

Card 10—Outcome: This card represents where the situation is heading and if/how the issue will be resolved if the querent continues their current course of action. Keep in mind, always, that the outcome is not set in stone; your client can always make changes to their situation and, thus, change the outcome.

So there you have it! The Celtic Cross in a nutshell. Now, there are many versions of the Celtic Cross spread, including differences in the order of the cards, but the version above is the one I use. Feel free to experiment and choose what works best for you.

Now that you've got a good understanding of the positions and their meanings, let's dig into how the cards interact with each other in the Celtic Cross spread.

Mastering the Celtic Cross: Exploring the Dynamics Between the Tarot Cards

This is where things get interesting! When we look at the dynamics between the Tarot cards in the Celtic Cross spread, exploring the reading's story, we can gain powerful (and even transformational) insight. And that's where the magic happens!

First, let's imagine the Celtic Cross split into two main sections: the Circle/Cross-section on the left (Cards 1 to 6) and the Staff section on the right (Cards 7 to 10).

The Circle/Cross shows what is going on in the querent's life at the time of the reading. This section is made up of two crosses—a central one (Cards 1 and 2) nested within a larger cross (Cards 3 to 6). The smaller cross represents the heart of the matter—what is most central to the querent at the time of the reading. The larger cross consists of two lines that overlay, the smaller cross.

The horizontal line (Cards 1, 3 and 4) shows time moving from the past on the left into the future on the right. The vertical line (Cards 1, 5 and 6) is the querent's consciousness moving from the unconscious on the bottom to the conscious mind on the top. Together these six cards give a snapshot of the inner and outer environment at the time of a reading.

The Staff section shows the relationship between the querent and the environment in which they operate, and can provide a better indication of what is happening in the broader context.

Still with me? Good! Now let's look at the following Tarot card combinations to build the story:

Compare the "Above" and "Below" cards (Cards 5 and 6). Is there a synergy between the conscious and the subconscious levels? Is there alignment between what is driving your client and what they aspire to? If yes, great—it will be a lot easier to resolve the issue. If not, then ask your client to reflect on the gap between what is influencing them on a deeper, subconscious level (Below) and what they are creating and aspiring to in their day-to-day life (Above).

Compare the "Above" and "Outcome" cards (Cards 5 and 10). Again, is there alignment between what the querent wants to happen and what will happen? Are they helping or hindering the situation? If you find that Cards 5 and 10 are opposing, then ask your client how they can actually create the outcomes they most desire. Look to the Advice card (Card 7) for guidance on what actions to take.

Compare the "Future" and "Outcome" cards (Cards 4 and 10). How are the events of the near future contributing or influencing the overall outcome? If there is a misalignment, ask the client how they can better manage these events to create their desired outcomes? Again, you can also refer to the Advice card (Card 7) for more detail.

Compare the "Below" and "Hopes/Fears" cards (Cards 6 and 9). If you are finding it difficult to interpret the Hopes/Fears, have a look at what is happening at the subconscious level within the querent (Card 6). Is there something in their subconscious realm that is creating fear or hope? If you see reversed cards in these positions, then it is likely the querent is not yet aware of their subconscious drivers and how they might be impacting them in the "real world."

Compare the "Advice" and "Outcome" cards (Cards 7 and 10). How did your client react to the outcome card? Do they seem unhappy? If so, remind them that they have the power to change the outcome by changing their current path. Take a look at the Advice card to see what actions the querent can take to create a more positive outcome. Also, take into consideration what events are likely to occur in the near future (Card 4) so that the querent can manage these effectively.

Then, bring it all together for deep insight into the situation at hand.

There is so much to learn by exploring the interactions between the cards in a Celtic Cross spread. Spend time practicing and playing with this essential spread, even if you're only reading for yourself – you'll be amazed at what you learn!

Activity

26.1 Practice the Celtic Cross Tarot Spread

- Complete a Celtic Cross reading for yourself.
- Journal your insights, paying particular attention to the dynamics between the cards.

Day 27: Reading Tarot for Yourself

Reading the Tarot cards for yourself is the perfect way to tap into your intuition and get the answers you need. Whether it's about deep spiritual matters or practical, day-to-day issues, the Tarot can help.

In this chapter, we'll put together everything you've learned so far and explore how to quickly and intuitively read your own Tarot cards so that you can access your inner wisdom, get crystal clear guidance and enrich your life every time you consult the Tarot.

Step 1: Create the Space

You might think a Tarot reading starts when you pick up the cards and shuffle them. But really, a Tarot reading begins from the moment you decide to consult the cards.

To create the most intuitive, clear readings for yourself, you need to create a sacred space for your reading.

Create the physical space by laying out your Tarot cloth, lighting a candle, burning some incense, or choosing your favorite crystals for the reading.

Create the mental space by clearing your mind and taking a few deep breaths to help you focus on the reading you're about to do.

Create the emotional space by letting go of any drama that you've been holding and opening your mind up to the possibility of discovering something new in the cards.

And finally, create the spiritual space by setting an intention for the reading and even calling in your guides, angels or Universal energy (whatever floats your boat!) to assist you in the reading.

Step 2: Get to the Heart of the Question

With a clear mind, ask yourself, "What do I really need to know right now?" For example, you might be feeling a lack of connection in your relationship with your partner. So, you might ask, "What do I need to know about my relationship right now?" or "How can I create more connection between my partner and myself?" Or, you might be wondering if you'll get that promotion you've been dreaming about. So, you ask, "What can I do to increase my chances of getting the promotion?" or "What is the energy surrounding this situation?"

Notice how these questions are phrased; you're not asking, "Will I get the job?" or "Will my relationship improve?" When you ask these kinds of questions, you're assuming your future is set in stone and there's little you can do to change it. But, as we know, that isn't true! Similarly, if you ask, "Should I go for the promotion?" you are assuming that the Tarot cards will make your decision for you. Never forget that you have free will and it is up to *you* to decide.

Finally, check in to make sure you're truly getting to the heart of the question. Hash out a few follow-up questions if you need to, and don't forget to determine why you're asking it. Make sure you're opening yourself up to that beautiful place of curiosity, empowerment, and manifestation. Once you have your question, write it down, so it's clear in your mind.

Step 3: Choose the Layout

Now that you have a clear question, it's time to choose the Tarot spread or layout you'll use.

I love using one of the simple three-card Tarot spreads we've discussed, such as:

- Past / Present / Future
- Situation / Problem / Advice

Or you might choose to create your own Tarot spread, based on what you're asking—or, you can simply choose to draw a few cards to see what comes through. The key is to make sure you're choosing a spread or layout that aligns with your question and will provide you the clarity you need.

Step 4: Shuffle and Lay Out the Cards

Now you're ready to pick up your cards and start shuffling. As you shuffle, channel your energy into the reading and focus on your question. When you feel ready, lay out the cards for your reading. Lay them side-by-side, from left to right, face-up.

Step 5: Read the Cards and Tell the Story

This is the fun part! Go through each card, from left to right, and interpret what it means for you.

Start by looking at the card and pay attention to the energy of the card and any intuitive hits you might receive right off the bat. Look at the picture and start describing what you see. What's happening and what's the story? And, how does it relate to you right now?

Once you have interpreted each card, look at all the cards in the Tarot reading, as if they were pages of a storybook. What story are the cards telling you?

Step 6: Answer Your Question

Now, go back to your original question and answer it based on what you have explored within the cards. (Trust me, some people forget to do this important step, especially if they're getting carried away with all the possible meanings of the cards!)

Step 7: Reflect

Write down the complete reading in your notebook, including the question you asked, the cards you pulled, your interpretations, and your answer.

Then, in a few weeks or even a few months, come back to the reading and reflect on the messages you received and what actually transpired. This reflection is a great way not only to develop your Tarot reading skills but also confirm and validate your intuition.

Those are the essential steps of any reading, but there are a few more things I want you to consider when reading for yourself. (Because, let's face it, we're human...)

Watch Out! Avoid These Traps When Reading for Yourself

Reading Tarot for yourself can end up being very confusing and inaccurate, especially when you may be making some critical mistakes (or if you're trying to land on a specific answer—hey, we've all done it!). Here are six common mistakes that can pop up when reading Tarot for yourself and how you can avoid them.

Mistake #1: You do a Tarot Reading When You're Highly Emotional

Your boyfriend rang to break up with you, and now you want to draw a few Tarot cards to see if you will get back together. You've lost your job in a major restructure, and you want to know when you'll get a new one. You've had a major argument with your best friend, and you want to know if you'll ever be friends again.

In all of these situations, your emotions are running high, and you're probably very worked up about what has happened. Reading Tarot for yourself in these types of circumstances is much more likely to result in an inaccurate or misdirected reading, especially as you're so emotionally invested. What you want is to be able to remain objective, calm and focused during a personal Tarot reading, so if something has happened and you are still very emotional about it, either wait until the initial reaction passes or consult an objective third party such as a professional Tarot reader.

Mistake #2: You Keep Drawing Extra Tarot Cards as "Clarifiers"

Sometimes, it makes sense to draw an extra Tarot card in a reading to clarify another card. For example, if you draw the Two of Swords, which is about making a decision between two options, you may want to draw another two cards to understand your options. That's fine—it makes sense, and it helps the cause.

But sometimes you draw a clarifying card, and then another, and another until you finally see something you like. What happens is that you end up with so many Tarot cards and different messages that it's unclear what the cards are actually trying to tell you. Or, you end up dissatisfied with the reading because you don't like what it's telling you. So, when reading Tarot for yourself, commit to drawing clarifying cards *only when you really need to or when it makes sense*. And even then, only draw one or two extra cards.

Mistake #3: You Do Multiple Tarot Readings on the Same Topic

One of the biggest mistakes I see other Tarot enthusiasts make is that they read over and over again on the same topic. "First, I did a Celtic Cross to see if we'd get back together, and then I did a Past/Present/Future Tarot spread, so I did another Celtic Cross just to make sure. The next day, I did a Horseshoe spread plus my daily love card..." and so on. No wonder people end up so confused about what the Tarot cards are trying to tell them!

Whenever any of my clients request a Tarot reading on the same topic within a short period, I strongly recommend that they do not go ahead with it. Instead, I tell them, "Wait at least a month before reading on the same topic, or at least until something significant changes."

It is the same with reading Tarot for yourself. Make a commitment now to read once and once only on your particular topic. Take note of the Tarot reading, then put it away and come back to it later.

Mistake #4: You Research Multiple Tarot Card Meanings for the One You Want

As we now know, Tarot cards do not have a single, universal meaning. If they did, you could get a computer to do your readings for you and call it a day! Instead, the cards are rich, complex, nuanced and, yes, open for interpretation. And that's a good thing!

However, that also means you might feel tempted to research lots of different Tarot card meanings until you find the one you want. When reading for yourself, you might ignore the most common meanings for a Tarot card (or what your intuition is telling) and hone in on a single sentence that gives the message you want.

Resist the temptation to go trawling for a Tarot card meaning that fits your hopes and desires. Instead, go with your gut. What does your gut say about what this Tarot reading is telling you? What is your initial reaction? Note it down and move on. Don't get stuck on trying to find the perfect, most convenient meaning.

Mistake #5: You Use a Complicated Tarot Spread

You want to know whether you should go to the wedding, so you turn to the Tarot spread that is the most popular—the Celtic Cross. But suddenly you're finding out about what happened in the past, what other people think about the situation, what you're hoping for, and your underlying fears, when all you really wanted to know was the potential outcome of turning up at a wedding!

Go back to basics! A one-card Tarot reading is amazingly powerful, particularly if you truly meditate on that card and go deep into its meaning and significance. And for many questions, you simply need a few Tarot cards, and you will have your answer. So, avoid using long and complicated readings, which only open up the path for more confusion and convoluted interpretation.

Mistake #6: You Interpret Your Tarot Reading the Way You Want

The hardest thing about reading Tarot for yourself is that you can end up with a "convenient" but highly subjective interpretation of the Tarot cards. When you are already emotionally invested in a situation, you will have your own perspectives and beliefs shaping your interpretation of the cards. In fact, it can be very hard to remain objective and professional about your own Tarot reading, particularly when you have a vested interest in its message.

There's nothing wrong with interpreting your own Tarot cards, but you may also want to seek the opinion of an objective third party. The Biddy Tarot Community is a great place to connect with fellow Tarot lovers who are happy to help! Remember, you can try the Biddy Tarot Community for 14 days for only $1! Go to **biddytarot.com/community-trial** to get started.

Reading Tarot for yourself can be incredibly powerful and insightful if you do it correctly. By avoiding these six mistakes, you will be well on your way to creating accurate Tarot readings for yourself.

Activity

27.1. Set Boundaries for Reading for Yourself

- Knowing what you know now, what do you commit to do and not to do when reading Tarot for yourself? Where will you draw a line in the sand?

Day 28: Reading Tarot for Others

Reading Tarot for clients is an exhilarating experience. You may feel a bit nervous about conducting a reading for someone else (particularly a stranger), but rest assured: this is a perfectly natural feeling that we all experience when we start reading Tarot. However, reading Tarot for clients is the fast track to overcoming those nerves and growing your confidence as a Tarot reader.

Now, when I say "clients," I mean anyone you're reading for; your clients could be your friends, your mom, your neighbor, or a paying client. I even recommend you treat yourself as a client when you do your own readings! Getting yourself into the "client" mindset when conducting your readings (even for your mom) will increase your confidence and prepare you for later down the track when you may choose to read for others professionally. Even if you don't, you'll find you get a lot more from your readings and connect with the cards on another level when you treat every querent as a client.

Here's what you need to keep in mind as you read Tarot for others.

Take Yourself Out of the Equation

Whether you're reading for a stranger or someone you know well, it is important to keep your personal energy and opinions out of the reading. Just as you learned in Day 22: Create a Sacred Space, you need to clear your mind and energy so that you can be fully present to receive the cards' messages. If you head into the reading still stewing about what your boss said to you in the meeting this morning, you won't be open to connecting with the client, the cards, and your intuition. You may even impact the reading with your energy.

Likewise, if your best friend asks what she should do to win her ex back, and you think her ex is a loser and she should never see him again, it may be easy to color the reading with your opinion. That's why you need to clear your mind and treat your bestie as though she is a paying client. Open a dialogue and ensure that you're getting to the heart of the question, then read the story in the cards as it presents itself (not as you'd like it to).

Set Clear Boundaries

As the Tarot reader, it's your role to set clear expectations of what you can and can't do in your reading. Let each client know upfront, before they even ask a question, that you don't do third party readings (that is, you can't tell him what his wife is thinking or intending to do), you won't give medical, financial or legal advice, and you certainly can't predict lotto numbers, baby names, or marriage proposals. Explaining a bit about what the Tarot is (and isn't) and how you work as a Tarot reader, will save a lot of time and frustration in the long run, while also enhancing the experience for the client.

Ask Empowering Questions

Due to the common misconceptions around what the Tarot can and cannot do, many clients will likely ask disempowering and closed questions, such as "When will I get a new job?" There's a belief that Tarot will 'tell the future', but you and I both know that there is so much more to Tarot than fortune-telling! So, if your client asks a question that doesn't feel like a great fit for a reading, simply work with them to rephrase the question. Talk to her about why you need to rephrase and agree on a more empowering alternative. And ask whether she thinks she'll still get the insight she needs from the question you've agreed to before you proceed with the reading. It will pay off in the end!

It's OK to Let People Touch Your Cards

A lot of people ask if it's OK to let the client touch your cards. This is perfectly fine *as long as you're comfortable with it*. While there may be some energetic transfer, this is actually a good thing. The client can shuffle the deck while concentrating on the query and infuse it with the true energy surrounding the question.

Create a Conversation with Your Client

The best Tarot readings are a co-creation between the reader and the client. This means inviting the client to participate, rather than be a passive recipient of your insights and information. Ask your clients questions throughout the reading and invite them to share what they see in the cards. Establishing a dialogue will result in a far more in-depth reading and leave the client far more satisfied with the results. (And remember, there are lots of beautiful and effective ways to clear and cleanse your deck between readings!)

Empower the Client with Recommended Actions

Ensure that your client leaves the reading feeling empowered and energized to create positive change. Let them know that no card is "good" or "bad" and that there are always light and shade and good advice with each Tarot card. Look to the cards and provide recommended actions the client can take to get the desired outcomes.

To wrap up the reading, I often ask the client to draw one last card to provide some final insight into the situation or guidance on what the current life lesson is. You can also use Oracle cards for this purpose.

Ask for Feedback

Constructive feedback from a trusted source is an absolute gift when it comes to developing your Tarot-reading confidence. The more you can understand how your readings impact your clients, and how your style resonates with different people, the faster you will grow.

There are several ways to ask for feedback (and ideal times to do so), which we'll cover in the next section.

Activity

28.1 Conduct a Tarot Reading for a Client

- Book in a reading with a friend or relative, and treat it is an appointment.

- After the reading, ask your client how it resonated for them.

- Write about your experience in your Tarot journal, including how your own reflection of the reading and the client's feedback were similar or different.

Day 29: Reflect and Ask for Feedback

The idea of asking someone for feedback may feel uncomfortable and bring up some resistance, but I promise that the more you do it, the more resilient you'll become and the better your Tarot readings will be. Plus, I guarantee that you will, more often than not, be delighted with the information you receive.

Feedback from a trusted source is an essential element of any growth process. Note that I say "trusted" source. If your aunt thinks Tarot is the work of the Devil, she's not the best person to ask! And, honestly, sometimes you don't even need to consider feedback from the client who was insistent that you tell her exactly when her ex will dump his pregnant wife and come back to her (and didn't like you trying to reframe her question into something more empowering). Those are not trusted sources—but can you guess what is perhaps your *most* trustworthy source?

It's your own intuition! By reflecting on your readings (those you do for yourself, plus those you do for others), you will fast-track your learning and improve a bit more every time you lay the cards out.

In this chapter, I'll show you how to collect useful feedback that can help you grow as a Tarot reader.

How to Ask for Feedback

OK, so you're ready to ask for feedback, but it feels scary. Here are some things to keep in mind that will make it a smooth and helpful experience and ensure you get exactly what you need.

Get Clear on Your Goals

Before you ask for feedback, it's important to get clear on your goals. Doing so will allow you to ask your client specific questions that will give you more direct feedback. For example, if your goal is to create a coaching style of reading, you may ask questions such as:

- "Did you feel that you were effectively heard?"
- "Did you feel that I understood your query?"

- "Did you feel that you walked away with a clear set of actions?"

- "After our reading, do you feel that you can create your desired future?"

You also want to get clear on what you want to do with the feedback you receive. Why are you asking for feedback? It could be for personal growth, client care, to understand your strengths and weaknesses, or even to collect testimonials for the sales page on your website. You will ask different questions depending on how you intend to use the feedback. For example, if your intention behind asking for feedback is to enhance your level of client care, you will ask questions that center on your client and how they felt about the experience. If you're asking questions for a testimonial, here are four questions that are powerful:

- "How did you feel about the situation before your reading with me?"

- "How do you feel about the situation now?"

- "What has changed for you as a result of the reading?"

- "What have you been able to create or achieve as a result of the reading?"

By getting clear on your goals first, you will make sure that the feedback you receive is useful and workable.

When to Ask for Feedback

There are a few points at which it makes sense to ask for feedback. You don't need to request feedback at all these points (that might be a bit much), but if you can find a nice, organic way of touching base with your client at each of these points, you'll definitely get deeper insights.

During the Reading: You might ask, "How is this resonating for you? How does this sit for you? Is this connecting with you?" This is a fantastic way of just checking that your client is on board with the reading, that they're not feeling confused, that they have clarity, that they understand what you're saying, and that you're also helping them with the situation at hand.

Directly After the Reading: It's best to keep the questions general at this point, particularly if you're in a face-to-face situation, since the client will still be processing a lot of information from the reading. It takes at least a few days for a reading to settle in and integrate, and for the client to see how it fits in with their current circumstances.

Directly after the reading, you might ask, "Was this reading helpful to you?" Or if you're more of a coaching style, "Are you clear on what steps you need to take to resolve this situation?" This is a check-in point to determine whether the client is satisfied with the reading, and if there is anything you can clarify.

It's also a good opportunity to say, "This is just the beginning of the changes that may occur for you. Expect that over the next few days, this reading will process a bit more, and you may find that new insights emerge." You can tell them at this point that you'll check back in about a week to get more specific feedback from the reading. Ask, "Are you OK if I contact you?"

Five to Seven Days After the Reading: This is the point at which your readings have had the chance to settle in. It's particularly important if there were difficult messages in the Tarot reading or if you noticed your client was feeling a little resistance. Giving them some time to process will help them come into a more constructive (and less emotional or reactive) space.

One to Three Months After the Reading: This is great for customer care because it shows that you're thinking about your clients and that you care about what's going on for them. A couple of questions that you can ask are, "How are things going since our reading together?" Or you can be a bit more specific: "How is it going with communicating with your partner? Are you moving things forward?"

You might also want to ask what has changed or what new information has emerged from the Tarot reading. Remember that things evolve and what you might see in a Tarot reading today could take on a whole different path, depending on what your client does.

How to Deal with Negative Feedback

As I mentioned earlier, most times the feedback you receive will be positive. But, unfortunately, nobody is perfect—including you and me—and even the super-famous Tarot readers have their "off" days.

First, don't let those "off" days define you. Don't let them stop you from doing what you love and what you have been "called" to do. You can't please everyone, so focus on the clients who love your work and appreciate you for who you are. That said, here are three key steps to take when you receive "negative" feedback that will help you grow as a Tarot reader:

1. Revisit Your "Love Letters"

I keep a "Love Letter" file in my inbox. It's jam-packed full of love and appreciation from all the wonderful feedback and comments from my Tarot reading clients, students, and visitors to my website. If I ever have a bad day or a dissatisfied client, the first thing I do is go to my Love Letter file and spend several minutes reminding myself of the 99.9% of people who really do love my work.

So, if you don't already have a Love Letter file, create one now and fill it up with loads of loving, appreciative comments from your clients. Then, when you do get negative feedback, go straight to love letters and remind yourself how amazing you really are.

2. Choose One Lesson

Knowing that you have something worthwhile to offer through your Tarot readings, now go back over the negative feedback. Pick out one thing you're going to do differently or that you have learned from the experience—*just one thing*.

For example, I had a client once who was upset that I didn't answer her specific question in the reading. She wanted to know what her ex really thought about her and the relationship. For me, this was outside of my ethical boundaries, so I looked at how she was in a relationship with her ex and what she might expect from the relationship moving forward. But she was not happy with the reading because I didn't give her the information she was looking for.

My one lesson from this experience was that I needed to be on the same page as my client before I started the reading. It didn't mean I would compromise my ethics, however, and read on something that I wasn't comfortable doing. So, I committed to changing all of my Tarot readings from that point forward. I now create and then share the customized Tarot spread with the client before the reading to make sure we have a mutual agreement of what is going to be covered.

Now, if a client feels that the spread doesn't cover their question, we can address it before the reading begins. Sometimes I change the spread, or other times I have an open discussion about what's OK to ask the Tarot and what's not. As a result, I have much happier clients. So, choose just one lesson you will take away from the experience and implement this lesson in your Tarot practice.

3. Close it Out with the Client

It's tempting to get into a long discussion with your client, either defending your Tarot reading or apologizing profusely for not meeting their needs. But, please, resist.

Instead, write a short note to the client thanking them for their honest feedback. Let them know what you've decided to improve or change and then wish them well on their journey.

No back-and-forth emails; just one short note. Why? Well, I don't know about you, but I much prefer to spend time with people who love what I do and who are ready and willing to exchange positive and uplifting energy. When I engage with someone who is giving out negative energy, it doesn't feel great. It's not that I want to avoid negative feedback altogether—it's actually very important to learn from these experiences. It's just that I don't want that negative energy to hang about, so I deal with it quickly and move forward. You might like to try the same.

In the next chapter, I'll talk you through how to deal with some of the other pitfalls that can come with reading Tarot for others—but the core message is the same: no matter what goes wrong, remember that you're great, then choose your lesson, learn from it, and move forward.

Activity

29.1 Seek Out Feedback After a Reading

- After you've completed a reading for someone else, reflect on your impressions of the reading in your Tarot journal.

- One week after the reading, send a personalized follow-up note to the client, asking how they're feeling after the reading, and if they could share some feedback with you on how the reading resonated for them, what they loved, and anything they can think of that would have improved the experience for them.

- When you receive the feedback, clear your mind and center your energy. Then, compare the client's feedback with your own notes and impressions. Journal on any insights that will help you improve your readings.

Day 30: Help! What If...

In this almost-final lesson, I want to spend a little more time talking about the things that might trip you up as a Tarot reader and how you can move past them as you grow and improve.

And we're going to start with the most insidious little trap of them all: self-doubt.

How to Deal with Self-Doubt

Self-doubt always shows up as a niggling (but persistent) voice. Let it chatter for too long, and self-doubt can drown out the voice of your intuition—and that's the last thing we want! Here are a few common doubts the Biddy Tarot community has shared and that I've struggled with myself:

I Barely Understood the Reading!

Sometimes a Tarot reading won't make perfect sense—it happens! It doesn't mean the reading is wrong or that you messed up along the way; it could just mean that you (or your client) aren't ready for the message just yet.

I recommend you write down your insights in your Tarot journal, even if you don't understand them. Maybe even fold over the corner of the page, or set a reminder in your phone to come back to your reading in a week or a month to see if it resonates a bit more.

I'm Not Happy with the Answer

Sometimes you may receive a message that is challenging to hear. For example, the cards may show that there are deep-seated issues in what you thought was a dreamy relationship.

Go back to why you asked about your relationship. Perhaps your subconscious mind knew something was up, but it's taking your conscious mind a little longer to catch up.

Get curious and open up to explore whatever comes up in a reading, even the darker shadows. If the cards are showing you something you haven't realized yet, be ready to go deeper and ask what it's all about. Draw more Tarot cards if you need a little more support.

Is It Possible I'm Making This Up?

Is that your intuition talking? Or is it a combo of your ego, fears, biases, and influence from that documentary you watched the other night? Sometimes it can be hard to tell the difference.

Do the work upfront to clear your mind and connect with your intuition, and you can trust that your reading will reflect your intuition.

If your mind is scattered and noisy when you perform the reading, then it's possible that you had some interference going on. Reflect on the experience and note down in your Tarot journal whether you veered from your usual routine or were distracted. Be honest with yourself, too, about whether you went "hunting" for an answer you liked, pulled twenty "clarification" cards, or cherry-picked card meanings to shape a certain message.

Now that we've addressed the self-doubt that can hold you back in your Tarot readings, it's time to move onto the next issue that may be keeping you from growing as a Tarot reader: difficult clients.

How to Deal with Difficult Clients

Dealing with difficult clients can sap our energy and leave us feeling down and depleted.

But it doesn't have to be that way. In fact, there are some very positive ways to deal with difficult clients, without having to run and hide every time you see their email come through or their phone number come up.

Here are a few common types of difficult clients, and some tips on how to handle them:

The "Not Possible" Client

A client comes to you for a relationship reading, and you have to break some bad news: "From what I'm seeing here, the relationship is well and truly over." Her response is, ahem, less than ideal:

"Nope. Not possible. He loves me."

You reply, "I understand you're hurting right now, but the Ten of Swords is showing me that this relationship has come to an end."

She still isn't having it and retorts, "You've got it all wrong. He loves me, and we're going to be together. I don't care what you say."

And you're secretly thinking, "Then why the hell did you just pay $50 for a reading!?"

No amount of reasoning is going to change this client's thinking. She has a very clear idea in her head about what's happening, and if anyone offers something different to that, it will fall on deaf ears. You may be best to say, "It sounds like you already have a pretty good sense of the situation, and you already have the answers you need, just by listening to your gut. Shall we move on to another topic?"

The Skeptic

"What would you like to know?" you ask your client.

To which he responds, "You tell me. You're the psychic." Oookay.

This is a little like walking into a doctor's appointment and saying, "Right, doc, tell me what's wrong with me," with no mention of what hurts or that the other day you blacked out and hit your head. No. Instead, what you're asking the doctor to do is to spend the first 50 minutes of your hour-long appointment running diagnostics until she can find the source of the issue. It's a complete waste of time and resources. You wouldn't do it, and the doctor wouldn't stand for it. Nor should you put up with it as a Tarot reader.

Ask your client to focus in on one area that's important to them. What keeps them up at night? What are they most uncertain about right now? Then focus the reading on that.

If your client still isn't giving anything away, suggest that you could spend the majority of your session together trying to isolate key concerns, but that this probably wouldn't tell them anything they don't know. What's going to be of more value is if you can identify a key concern up front and spend the rest of the session delving deeper into what the client really needs to know and how they can manifest the best outcomes.

The "Eeyore" Client

Reader: "I suspect it will be a challenging few months ahead for finding work. But what the Two of Wands suggests is that it may be time to step outside your comfort zone. How about applying for work in a new city?"

Client: "That'd never work."

Reader: "OK, how about applying for roles in a different industry?"

Client: "No way. They'd never hire me."

Reader: "Ah, let's draw another advice card. OK, how about asking your friends if they know of any vacant roles (Three of Cups)?"

Client: "I could never ask my friends for work."

You could try to convince this client until you're blue in the face that there are many opportunities available, but no matter how much of a positive spin you put on things, they're not listening.

My advice...

Present your client with 2 or 3 different options for what they can do to improve their situation. Write them down and give the piece of paper to your client. Suggest that they come back to those recommendations in the next 1-2 weeks. They may be more open to the possibilities after some time has passed.

The Repeat Client

Your client wants to know, "Will I get back with my ex?"

(Three days later...)

"Will I get back with my ex?"

(Two days later...)

"Will I get back with my ex?"

Apparently, a lot can happen in five days.

The trouble here is that the "repeat" client is often just fishing for the answer they want or sweating over the small stuff. The more you offer to read for them, the more you are fueling the fire.

And while an unscrupulous reader will see this as an opportunity to make a quick buck (it's sad, but true), this is your opportunity to make a lasting, positive, and ethical impression.

Whenever a client asks me for a repeat reading, I say, "I don't feel comfortable reading for you on this topic again in such a short stretch of time. It's not valuable to you, and it's not valuable to me, because we'll simply see the same message coming up. I strongly recommend that you give it at least 4-6 weeks or until something significant has changed before we have another Tarot reading."

The "It Ain't Happening" Client

A client marches into their appointment with you and snaps, "You told me that I would have sold my house by now. Well, I haven't." This is why I feel very uncomfortable doing purely predictive readings. I am a strong believer that we do not have pre-defined futures and that we can exercise our free will to make decisions that will, in turn, change our futures.

That's why I prefer to focus on what the client can do to achieve their most desired outcome, rather than give a pre-defined picture of what will and won't happen.

If you have provided a prediction, and it hasn't yet manifested, suggest that the prediction may have a longer timeframe. Oftentimes, readings are "valid" for 6-12 months. Gently remind your client that her decisions can influence the outcomes, and if she would like things to move faster, she may need to take more action.

Also, a question to the Tarot cards such as, "What indicators will I see when [desired event] is about to happen?" can be a helpful way of predicting when something will happen, without tying it to an actual date.

The "It's an Emergency" Client

You get a panicked email from a client: "I need a reading RIGHT NOW."

I know there are times when it feels like we need guidance and insight RIGHT NOW. But these are often times when we're feeling highly emotional and scattered. It may be more constructive for your client to write down his thoughts and feelings, meditate or talk it over with a friend first. Then, consult a Tarot reader or a professional who can help.

You can protect yourself against "emergency" Tarot readings by simply having a booking system or a wait list. Indicate to your client the days or weeks you're available and that you'd love to be able to read for them then. If you're sensing they're highly emotional, reconnect a day before the reading to check in on any developments.

Activity

30.1 Turn Self-Doubt into Self-Love

- Take some time in your sacred space with your Tarot journal to reframe the limiting beliefs you've been feeding yourself about your Tarot reading skills.

- Write a list of all the self-doubt thoughts you've experienced as you've worked through this book. For example, maybe you skipped the chapter on reading for others, because you told yourself that you didn't know enough yet. Or perhaps you practiced the Celtic Cross and wondered if what you were writing in your journal was actually your intuition speaking, or just your imagination running wild.

- Now, reframe each of these doubts in the positive. For example, "it's just my imagination" could turn into "my intuition speaks to me through my imagination".

- Finally, write down what action you will take every time one of these doubts pops up in your Tarot readings. Maybe if you're doubting your intuition during a reading, you can commit to taking a centering breath and picturing white light flowing through your crown chakra, infusing you with intuition. Having these anchors to bring you back to self-love will help you connect back to your intuition and stay present in the reading.

Day 31 : Trust Your Intuition

Well, here we are! Day 31! And if there's one message I want you to take with you as you continue to learn and grow as a Tarot reader, it's this: *trust your intuition.*

Your intuition bridges the gap between the conscious and subconscious parts of your mind, and it's the voice of your Higher Self. In fact, Carl G. Jung, a well-known psychotherapist and spiritualist, theorized that intuition...

- Is a natural part of all of us;
- Works within us to help us understand ourselves;
- Enables us to understand others; and
- Connects us to a larger metaphysical awareness that spans the whole of time and space called the collective unconscious.

Pretty amazing, right?

Yet trusting our intuition remains one of the biggest challenges in learning Tarot. Here's what just a few of my Facebook followers had to say about learning to trust their intuition:

> **"The main problem that I had with Tarot was knowing when to let go of the books and to follow my own GUT feel."**

> **"For me, it was letting go of the rules and allowing my intuition to guide me. When I first started, I got stuck worrying about how I "should" be reading the cards."**

> **"My biggest challenge was believing in myself."**

Learning to trust your intuition is essential to reading the Tarot—and it's imperative if you are to go from being an amateur Tarot reader to a professional. Anyone can look up the meanings of the Tarot cards and select the interpretation that suits them best. But it takes a truly confident and intuitive reader to read between the lines and weave a story within the cards. Your intuition is the key to bringing your Tarot readings to life and learning what they have to say.

Developing Your Intuition in Between Readings

Developing and trusting your intuition takes time. But the more you connect with your intuitive self, the easier it will become and the more natural it will feel. Here are a number of practical methods for developing your intuition in between Tarot readings.

Practice Silence

One of the best techniques I learned from one of my favorite books, Eckhart Tolle's *The Power of Now*, was to quiet the mind and listen for the silence. This is highly effective in clearing away all of that chatter in our minds and creating space to allow for our inner voice to come through. Before every Tarot reading, I stop to listen to the silence.

Meditate on a Tarot Card

Just as you learned on Day 21, you can meditate with your Tarot cards to access your subconscious knowledge of that card. Select one Tarot card and place it in front of you. Allow your mind to clear, and then observe what images, feelings, or energies come to you during this time. Try to forget about traditional meanings and instead focus on what you are sensing from this card.

Listen to your Dreams

Dreams are an excellent source of subconscious information. By keeping a dream journal, you can begin to see the patterns between your dreams and your reality. If you have a pressing question, meditate on it before falling asleep, and in the morning when you wake up, write down what you dreamed. No doubt you will have the answer to your question.

Using Your Intuition During a Tarot Reading

Using your intuition during a Tarot reading is one of those things that works well when you're not really trying to do it. And when you are trying to be intuitive, it often makes it a lot more difficult or forced. So, first, relax, breathe, and pause before you start a Tarot reading. See what comes. Here are a few more things you can do to make sure you're tapping into the voice of your intuition—and build your trust in what it has to say.

Pay Attention to Your First Reactions

Listen carefully to what you "hear" during a Tarot reading. A phrase or a word may suddenly come to mind without any real explanation, or you may literally hear a voice that gives you a message. Pay attention to what you see in a Tarot card or a reading, too. Where is your eye drawn? What color, object, person, or shape is grabbing your attention? What does this tell you about the reading or the situation?

Dig into your emotions during a reading. Do you feel genuinely happy and joyous when you see the cards in front of you? Or do you have a strange, nagging suspicion that something isn't right? What's your personal state of mind? What might this be telling you about your client's situation? Different people will pick up different energies from a reading. Some people are clairaudient (clear hearing), some are clairvoyant (clear seeing), some are clairsentient (clear feeling) and some are claircognizant (clear knowing). You might be one of these or many. Simply pay attention to all possible senses for subtle messages during a reading.

Call It as You See It

Sometimes a message will come to you during a reading that may not make any sense. Trust it. Say what you see, even if it seems "out there." Have faith in the cards. Just because you may not understand what you are being shown, there is a reason why you are seeing, hearing, or feeling it. Relax, take a breath, and the message will come to you.

And anyway, what's the worst thing that could happen? You could be wrong. It's OK. Acknowledge it and move on. What's worse is if you do sense something and you never mention it, only to find out months later that your intuition was indeed right.

Use the "No Spread" Spread

Rather than using a defined Tarot spread, next time you have a question, start with one card. Concentrate on the card and what it is telling you and use it to shape your next question. Continue doing this until you feel clear on what you need to do about your concern.

Practice Reading Aloud

It may seem a little strange at first, particularly if you're reading for yourself, but interpreting your Tarot reading aloud will help you immensely in developing and trusting your intuition.

Often, when we verbalize something, the words and the thoughts come more freely.

So, say what you see in the cards—what stories you see, what messages you pick up on, what you are feeling at the time, what you hear in your mind. Speak up! Even better, grab a microphone and record yourself doing a reading. (This is also an excellent way to keep track of your readings.)

When I was an online Tarot reader, this is one aspect I missed! However, on the odd occasion when I did readings face-to-face, I could feel the energy rushing through me as I interpreted the reading out loud. The words flowed, and I found myself completely connected to a Higher Power and my intuition. My eyes would light up, my hands would start waving, and I'd be completely "in the zone"!

Get Feedback

One of the best ways to gain confidence and trust in your own intuition is to find out if your "hunch" was on target or not.

During a reading, create a dialogue with your client, checking in to see if your intuitive feelings are right. You might want to say something like, "I'm seeing this—does this resonate?" or "I'm getting this—does this have meaning for you?" After a reading, find out if your interpretation matched reality. Check in with your client a few days after the reading and, if possible, a few months after. The more positive feedback you get, the more you will trust that niggling feeling you have during a reading, no matter how whacky or "out there" it might be.

Activity

31.1 Pick a Card, Any Card

- Select a card randomly from your Tarot deck.

- Now, using your intuition only, interpret the card and what it means for you for the rest of the day. Don't even think about picking up a book for this activity!

- Verbalize what you see, what you hear, and what you feel in the card laid out in front of you. (Even better, record yourself.) Don't hold back. Say every thought out loud as it occurs to you. As you finish speaking one thought, listen for the next one.

- What images stand out to you? What thoughts, memories, phrases, feelings, and messages does it elicit? Say it out loud.

- What jumps out at you? What does it say to you? Say it out loud.

- Keep speaking aloud as different messages come to you, freely and without judgment. It doesn't matter if you go off on a tangent—go with it and see where it takes you.

- After a few minutes, stop and note down the key messages from your intuitive reading of the card.

- Now, if you want to find out if your intuition is indeed accurate, take note throughout your day how these intuitive feelings manifest. Check back in at the end of the day and see how well your intuition has guided you.

Where to From Here?

Can you believe we've already reached the end?? Congratulations on devoting at least 31 days to your Tarot study! By now, you can intuitively interpret the Tarot cards in simple readings for yourself and others, and you're on the way to becoming a talented Tarot reader!

However, the journey doesn't end here. In fact, a whole new world of Tarot is opening up to you right now. You're tapping into the energy of The Fool, who finds himself stepping into a new possibility as he embarks on the journey through the lessons of the Major Arcana. There are so many exciting things to come.

So, where to from here?

Stay Focused and Remember to Breathe

When you start learning something new, it's easy to become daunted by everything you have to master to reach your final goal—and Tarot is no exception! With 78 Tarot cards and a raft of different scenarios and possible meanings, the concept of doing an accurate Tarot reading without a book by your side might feel impossible.

This is why focus is critical.

First, it helps you pay attention to the task at hand so you don't become paralyzed by the thought of everything to follow.

Second, you have to focus so you can ignore all the possible distractions that are always waiting to take you off your path.

So, when you find yourself feeling overwhelmed, focus on just one Suit, or just the Court Cards, or just three-card spreads, or just reading on love and relationships. Start small and then grow from there. And remember to breathe – you've got this!

Don't Be Afraid to Make Mistakes

Fear of failure is often one of the biggest obstacles on the road to learning new things—and that's understandable! But you have to be willing to make mistakes to learn and grow. That's what practice is. The sooner you get comfortable making mistakes, the quicker you'll grow as a Tarot reader.

This is also critical in learning to trust your intuition. You have to start listening to your intuition and going with it. You probably won't be accurate 100% of the time, but at least you will learn from your mistakes and your "guesses." It is much better to guess at something than to hold back and regret it later.

Get to Know the Tarot Cards Like They're Your Best Friends

After reading this book, no doubt you have a good 'feel' for the Tarot cards and what they mean in a reading. However, know this – there is always more to discover with Tarot!

The more you practice your readings, the more stories and real-life examples you will have for each of the Tarot cards.

The more you do your Daily Tarot Card reading, the more you will connect on a personal level with your cards.

And the more you learn about the Tarot card meanings, the more insight you will bring to your readings. My book, The Ultimate Guide to Tarot Card Meanings, is a great place to get started. Take a peek at **biddytarot.com/ultimate-tarot**. And, if you want to master the Tarot card meanings, then check out my online Tarot course at **biddytarot.com/master-tarot**.

Develop Your Expertise and Experience

To become truly talented at reading Tarot for yourself and others, it's important you develop both your expertise (learning to read Tarot from books and courses) and your experience (real-world Tarot reading practice).

If you find yourself endlessly buried in the books, trying to become a master of Tarot, take a break and channel your time into reading Tarot for others instead. Through the experience of reading Tarot, you'll boost your confidence and, ultimately, your expertise. The Biddy Tarot Community is a great place to practice reading Tarot in exchange for feedback – you can try it out for only $1 at **biddytarot.com/community-trial**.

On the other hand, if you're only doing Tarot readings and not much else, then it may be helpful to dive into a few Tarot books and courses to truly hone your skills and develop your expertise. Even when you've been reading Tarot for 25+ years like I have, there's always something new to learn. (At Biddy Tarot, we offer some amazing Tarot courses to take your readings to the next level, including our signature Biddy Tarot Certification Program – find out more at **biddytarot.com/certificate**).

And finally... Thank you! Thank you so much for including me in your Tarot journey. I hope this is the beginning of your long and beautiful relationship with the Tarot and your inner wisdom.

With love and gratitude,

You're Invited to Join the Biddy Tarot Community for Only $1

Discover how to become a more confident, intuitive tarot reader inside the Biddy Tarot Community, with over 1500+ Tarot Lovers.

Inside the Community, you can:

- Practice reading Tarot for others on the Free Tarot Reading platform
- Join in the forum conversation with 1500+ Tarot enthusiasts
- Get answers to all of your questions as you develop your Tarot reading skills
- Learn from 25+ Tarot Topics and Masterclasses
- Access 50+ Tarot resources including spreads, charts and worksheets
- Boost your Tarot reading confidence and connect with your Tarot tribe

As a special thank-you for reading Intuitive Tarot and including me on your Tarot journey, you're invited to join the #1 online Tarot community for just $1 for 14 days.

Get started today at biddytarot.com/community-trial.

Gratitude

As well as thanking you, the reader, for coming along on this 31 Day journey with me, I want to thank the amazing team that helped me bring this book to life.

I offer my gratitude to...

My developmental editor, Ann Maynard, for making magic with the original words I put on the page. Ann, you are a true wizard.

Content assistant and copy editor Jen Martin, for reading every line a hundred times and making sure everything is exactly where it should be.

Illustrator Ellie Moreing, who brought my vision alive with her beautiful illustrations. Thank you, Ellie, for "getting it". Your gifts are inspiring.

Designer (and patient husband) Anthony Esselmont, for creating a beautiful new edition for our readers to enjoy. Thank you for your vision and bringing a fresh feel to this 31 Day journey.

The wonderful Biddy Tarot team, for their support, dedication, hard work and energy. You make this work a joy.

To our Biddy Tarot community, thank you for inviting me into your lives and being open to diving into the true potential of Tarot.

And again, I offer my gratitude to you, the reader. Thank you for exploring the Tarot and your intuition with me. I hope that you continue your intuitive Tarot studies and that our paths cross again sometime soon.

Appendix: Tools and Templates

Tarot Suit Summary

Suit   Element

Keywords/
Phrases

Positive
Aspects

Negative
Aspects

Day to Day
Activities &
Events

Personality
Types &
Characteristics

Images Associated with the Suit

Tarot Card Profile

Card   Card Image

Date

Element

Numerological
Association

Keywords/
Phrases

Story/
Description

General Tarot
Card Meanings

Context-specific Meanings

Career, Work & Finances   Spirituality

Personality Types   Well-being & Health

Relationships & Love   Other

A Card A Day

Card   Card Image

Date

Initial
Impressions

Keywords/
Phrases

What is happening in the card/picture?   What emotion is being expressed?

Symbols and Images that Stand Out   Greeting Card Message

Personal Experience (at the end of the day)

Events and Situations   People

Lessons Learned   New Insights

Three-Card Tarot Spread

Date   Client

Question   Card 1   Card 2   Card 3

Spread Used

Key Patterns/Themes during Reading   Significance of these Patterns

                     Card 1   Card 2   Card 3

Position

Keywords

Interpretation

Overall Story in the Cards

Answer to the Original Question   Advice or Recommendations

25 Easy Three-Card Tarot Spreads

Sure, there are tons of fancy (and complicated) Tarot spreads that have ten, twenty, even all seventy-eight Tarot cards in them. But if you want to get to the heart of your question, then the best place to start is with a simple three-card Tarot reading.

General Three Card Tarot Spreads

Past | Present | Future

The nature of your problem | The cause | The solution

Current situation | Obstacle | Advice

Situation | Action | Outcome

Context of the situation | Where you need to focus | Outcome

What I think | What I feel | What I do

Three-Card Spreads for the Future

Where you stand now | What you aspire to | How to get there

What you aspire to | What is standing in your way | How you can overcome this

What will help you | What will hinder you | What is your unrealized potential

Three-Card Spreads for Understanding the Past

What you can change | What you can't change | What you may not be aware of

What worked well | What didn't work well | Key learnings

Three-Card Spreads for Love and Relationships

You | The other person | The relationship

What you want from the relationship | What they want from the relationship | Where the relationship is heading

What brings you together | What pulls you apart | What needs your attention

Three-Card Spreads for Decision-Making

Strengths | Weaknesses | Advice

Opportunities | Challenges | Outcome

Option 1 | Option 2 | Option 3

Option 1 | Option 2 | What you need to know to make a decision

The solution | An alternative solution | How to choose

Three-Card Spreads for Self Discovery

Mind | Body | Spirit

Your conscious mind | Your sub-conscious mind | Your super-conscious mind

Material state | Emotional state | Spiritual state

You | Your current path | Your potential

Stop | Start | Continue

What the Universe wants you to be | The personal qualities required | Specific action required